"In punchy, [...] uss Stoddard offers both inspiratic [...] ocial enterprise movement. Bringing to bear both his considerable personal experience as well as key research and data, Stoddard manages to cover the case for, the fundamentals of, and success stories about the burgeoning field of social enterprises. Whether you are an aspiring entrepreneur, an employee, or a consumer (yup—basically anyone), this book is for you!"

KATE WILLIAMS
CEO, 1% for the Planet

"This is a rare, pull-back-the-curtain book for social entrepreneurs. Russ shares the secrets to creating authentic social, environmental, and financial impact including a myriad of practical ideas that you can implement TODAY. Want to use business as a force for good? Buy this book. You won't be sorry."

ANGELI WELLER
Director, Responsible Business Initiative at Boise State University

"Russ has been building purpose-driven, humane businesses longer than anyone I know. He embodies all that is right about business and life, and to have his collective wisdom down in print is a treasure. This book should be required reading for everyone. Employees can learn what to expect out of their employers, and leaders can learn how to shape their businesses in a thoughtful and meaningful manner."

PETE GOMBERT
Managing Director, GoodWell

RISE UP

How to Build a Socially Conscious Business

RUSS STODDARD

elevate

Published in Boise, Idaho, by Elevate, an imprint of Elevate Publishing
ISBN: 9781945449383
E-Book ISBN: 9781945449390
Library of Congress Control Number: 2017933782

ACKNOWLEDGMENTS

To Lisa Fisher, for pointing me in the direction of B Corporation certification.

To the people of B Lab, who developed the beautiful (and rigorous) structure for B Corporation certification—and for fueling a worldwide business movement.

To the kind, talented, and generous people I work with at Oliver Russell, who have taken teamwork and volunteering to new highs (and new worlds).

To our global community of social entrepreneurs, for whom the challenge of making a financial profit simply isn't enough.

To Antonia Chappell, my co-founder at Social Good Network, who urged me to write this book.

To Steve Hodges, a successful startup entrepreneur and all-star angel investor who was kind, wise, and steady in his support of Social Good Network.

To Jim Everett, a lifelong role model I've known through his leadership role at the Treasure Valley Family YMCA and now beyond.

To my Bell Buckle group of cohorts—you know who you are.

To Sally and Mary, who I promised a long time ago I would acknowledge when I published my first book. (It only took four decades.)

To my kids, Kate and Henry, Forest and Ruby—all grown up and blazing nontraditional, passionate paths in the world.

For my two moms, who gave and gave and gave.

And to Sarah, whose love, hard work, spirit of social justice, and care for those on the margins provide my daily inspiration.

CONTENTS

INTRODUCTION

I once had a prospective client say, "You're a bit of a different bird, aren't you, Russ?"

He was a big-time business guy, all about the bottom line. I thought about what he said when I went home that night, and I had to agree—in the world of business, I was a little bit different. Always had been, right from the start.

When you're adopted, as I was, your life begins with questions. It actually originates as a question mark for your parents: Should we keep this child? It's a question you didn't ask, but were born into.

That's what I'm contemplating as I sit on a hard bed in a hotel room in Missoula, Montana, the town of my birth in the now-long-ago year of 1958. I'm sneaking a day away from my office in Boise to begin writing this book about building a purpose-driven company, and I wonder: Could my birth here to a single mother on welfare, followed by adoption and a life of questioning my origins, have led to a lifelong narrative of seeking meaning through my work?

The typical origin questions fill my mind: Who am I? Who are my birth parents? Where are they? What are they doing right now, this very instant? Why do I look like I do—gangly, tall, awkward, with a long, stork-like neck and a head full of curly, blonde hair?

'WHY' ENTERS THE WORKPLACE
Why?

It's the most human of questions. Even as we work to secure our basic needs, such as food and shelter, we find ourselves looking up from this lowest rung of Maslow's hierarchy of needs, pointed toward the pinnacle of self-actualization, asking:

"Why?"

It's a question we ask of the past, especially as we ponder: Why does it have to be this way?

And in today's ever-changing workplace, the "why" question is increasingly finding a home. Business bestsellers are dedicated to the question. (*Start With Why* by Simon Sinek is a favorite example.) Millennials and subsequent generations are now asking the question of brands when considering their purchases—and when weighing their employment options.

Why?

And with that simple question, many in the business world are finding an answer.

A DAY IN THE LIFE
Your workday begins at 8 a.m., give or take. You grab a cup of coffee. Coworkers wander in, and you exchange stories. You check your email, the headlines, and maybe reply to a text message.

And then there's the work itself, yawning in front of you like a lazy river with a slight upstream breeze. Tasks that once challenged you, now mastered, have become mundane. Hey, no big deal—you're getting paid for this, right?

And then there are the episodic meetings, one stacked upon another, some even yielding the outcome of more scheduled meetings. The top-down, hierarchical reporting structure, the climb of the ladder, one rung at a time. And the paycheck, of course, delivered electronically twice monthly to cover the rent, kids' shoes, and an occasional dinner out.

And there's your day—your life—one day strung after another.

And at the end of this day? If you're like me, you wonder what you actually accomplished. Some days, it's hard to conjure anything that remotely resembles progress.

COMBINING PROFIT WITH PURPOSE

That feeling eventually led me to start my own company, Oliver Russell. Founded in 1991, my desire was to create a different type of business, one that gives back, a for-profit with an impetus to help nonprofits in the community. Who knows, perhaps that drive to give back came from my birth mother, Marilyn—whom I was fortunate to find later in life. She gave me to another set of parents because she loved me, providing the first innate, in-utero lesson in giving.

In the beginning, I shaped four core values for my fledgling business: to be creative, collaborative, progressive (which we define as moving forward by embracing change), and socially responsible.

For much of our first two decades in business, these values chiefly manifested themselves as funding for community nonprofits through a formal grant program. We helped protect wild spaces through conservation easements. We jump-started efforts to create a human-rights memorial. We even helped fund, in a small way, the U.S. Women's Olympic Fencing Team.

Through these efforts, which we measured along the way, we've now contributed more than $1.9 million in cash and services to various nonprofits.

That made the work more meaningful. But it wasn't enough.

MEASURING OUR IMPACT

In 2010, my friend Lisa Fisher, an activist in the world of social enterprise, told me about the creation of a new type of company, a B Corporation. She said these companies intentionally use their business models to solve social and environmental issues, and urged me to certify Oliver Russell as a B Corporation, a process involving a thorough review of a company's governance, policies, and operations.

At the time, I thought this would be fairly easy for us to achieve. After all, we were a progressive company that had always acted on our core value of social responsibility. I jumped at the chance to prove it against a third-party standard.

The first time we completed the assessment, however, we didn't meet the baseline score for certification. We were close, but hadn't cleared the minimum threshold score to become a B Corp. This was a little shocking to me, as I thought we were pretty stellar when it came to social responsibility. Little did I know!

This initial shock also conveyed that this certification wasn't a rubber stamp; it was the real deal. If we wanted to act upon our values, we needed to get our operations in line with this certification process. We revisited our assessment and adopted a number of changes to our environmental policies that enabled us to barely clear the bar and achieve the minimum score required to become a Certified B Corporation.

Our business has never been the same since. It's better, more fulfilling, and more challenging.

I am indebted to the people at B Lab, the nonprofit that runs the B Corporation certification process. They provided the foundation for much of our work toward building a purpose-driven business and many of the lessons I'll convey in this book.

For me, embracing a higher purpose in our business and codifying it through a certification process has made all the difference in the world. I now operate in an environment that truly creates the meaning I'm seeking from my work, and I believe that's also the case for my coworkers at Oliver Russell.

PEOPLE, PROFIT, AND PLANET

Now don't get me wrong—I still have my days. There are still far too many meetings, cash-flow challenges, and HR issues. But in these moments, I remind myself that I'm working for a triple-bottom-line business that promotes people, planet, *and* profit. (It's interesting to note "profit" is evolving in some quarters to the usage of "prosperity" with the intent of being more inclusive.) We've built a workplace recognized as one of the best in the world by B Lab and others. Our business model minimizes impact on the environment and propels our purpose-driven clients who provide products, services, and business models to benefit society.

In the course of a business day, we might work with an entrepreneur trying to provide healthy food to low-income communities. We may volunteer over the noon hour to rebuild trails in the nearby Boise foothills. Or we might strategize a crowdfunding campaign to help a person wrongfully convicted of murder (and who subsequently served a 22-year sentence), who's now in need of assistance.

You want an energy boost and a sense of meaning? There's your "Why." It's really as simple as that.

I hope the lessons I've learned, and the mistakes I've made—all of which I cover in this book—will help you create a socially conscious business that provides you and your team with a sense of meaning that's rewarding and sustaining.

So let's get on with it. Let's rise up and build something bigger and better, together.

"

"How you climb
a mountain is
more important
than reaching
the top."

Yvon Chouinard
Co-founder, Patagonia

CHAPTER 1
WHAT IS A SOCIAL ENTERPRISE?

Corporate social responsibility (CSR) is often used as an umbrella term for a business category including ideas such as social impact, corporate sustainability, purpose, and social responsibility.

Perhaps we should start by defining the subject of this chapter: What *is* a social enterprise? The definition can get a little confusing because the business world describes a social enterprise in a lot of different ways: purpose-driven companies, socially responsible companies, sustainable companies, conscious companies, socially conscious companies—well, you get the idea. Yes, some might sound a little new-agey, but don't mistake these terms for a lack of competitive commercial fire or drive for profit within the category. They just have a different, more sustainable way of creating it.

A working definition might tell you that CSR is a business approach to creating sustainable development by providing economic, social, and environmental benefits. For sure, that's saying all the right things, but I don't think CSR is the right classification for the new breed of company you'll be creating. To understand why I'm debating semantics here, let's quickly examine CSR's evolution to gain some context for the discussion.

THE RIGHT THING TO DO

The notion of CSR started with a fuzzy yet innate sense that this behavior was the right thing to do. And it was business people, rather than consumers, who initiated the idea of CSR.

Businesses have been concerned with society and social well-being for centuries, but modern-day CSR traces its initial roots to the 1940s and 50s, when *Fortune* first polled business executives about their social responsibilities and the book *Social Responsibilities of a Businessman* by Howard R. Bowen was published.

As time went on, the 70s introduced us to the notion of social responsibility as long-run profit maximization. During this period, the impetus driving corporate involvement with social good often stemmed from a defensive posture to mitigate risk.

Companies in the 70s acknowledged that poor corporate actions in the marketplace or workplace could negatively affect operations and reputation, and the resulting costs—direct or indirect—could affect profitability. Among others, these costs could stem from lawsuits, new governmental regulations, product recalls, or consumer boycotts.

DEFINING SOCIAL ENTERPRISE

These days, when entrepreneurs choose to start a social enterprise, they're decidedly on the offensive.

And that's the primary distinction we'll draw between CSR and social enterprise—the latter deliberately weaves purpose, social impact, and public benefit into its business model.

Many experts differ on what a social enterprise actually is, but here's the definition I use: a for-profit company that intentionally provides products, services, or business models that benefit society and/or the environment using commercial market strategies. Even this book could serve as an example of a product that benefits society. Its intent is to help guide and motivate other entrepreneurs pursuing social change, and a portion of its revenues will be used to fund grants and impact investments.

Today, social enterprises run the spectrum, from high-tech startups developing technology that promotes water conservation, to cooperative ventures of consumers banding together around common purposes, as is the case with health insurance co-ops. (There are nonprofits out there that also fit the model by virtue of adopting marketplace ideals and working to build earned revenue to augment—or replace—contributed revenue from grants and donations. Various government agencies could lay claim to social enterprise models as well.)

Social enterprise is still about the bottom line—just a different one. As a social enterprise, your company will work purposefully toward three general outcomes: social impact, environmental benefit, and financial profit.

Here's a brief overview of the basic social enterprise measuring sticks, and how your business will look as you work toward these outcomes.

ENVIRONMENT

For big companies that produce sustainability reports as part of their CSR initiatives, measuring environmental inputs and outputs might be old hat. But to newer or smaller businesses, this will likely change the way you think about your business. And if what I'm about to share invokes images of recycling programs, you're swimming in the shallow end. You'll be taking a deeper dive and measuring a number of your company's environmental impacts—from the waste stream you generate to your water and energy consumption. You'll also go further afield as you measure the impacts caused by your distribution channels and your business travel, and the environmental performance of your supply chain. And that's just for starters.

WORKERS

This measuring stick definitely doesn't come from the slash and burn philosophy of the old-school corporate sustainability book when human resources were largely viewed as being disposable. And if it harkens by name (workers) to the proletariat, it's because one of the largest social impacts a company can have is on the lives of the people who work there. How a business treats its employees has become increasingly important to consumers (not to mention a key recruiting and retention measure). It puts the emphasis squarely on people, and depending upon the methodology, you'll likely measure your relationship with your team through compensation ratios, benefits, health and safety practices, training, and ownership opportunities, as well as the overall corporate culture and work environment.

COMMUNITY

Historically, corporate concern for the community has been all about philanthropy. And while corporate contributions figure into a social enterprise, community becomes a bigger player on a much broader stage. You might actually design a product or service that directly benefits your community, such as an environmentally friendly lawn care product or a transportation service that helps segments of the community get to work. Beyond this, your contribution to community could also involve supplier relations, local-purchasing policies, and alternative transportation, among many others.

CUSTOMERS

Today, many social enterprises are formed completely around addressing a specific social or environmental problem for an underserved customer base. Do your products or services meet a unique need for low-income, minority, or other underserved populations? Are you helping organic farmers gain a foothold in the market through cooperative purchasing and marketing? Do you provide an alternative to big banks for small investors who want to pursue a relationship with a socially responsible financial services company? For many social enterprises, the customer *is* their purpose. And we're not talking tired corporate adages such as "The customer is always right" here.

GOVERNANCE

I know. Corporate governance. Boring, right? Not in the realm of social enterprise. There are a number of innovative developments and practices on this front that pertain to social enterprises. New legal structures are coming into play that not only give you protections to act as a social enterprise, but also require you to formally demonstrate the public benefit you are creating. These legal structures require a level of heightened transparency, including making your corporate practices and policies readily available to your stakeholders and the public at large. We'll cover a few of these options in more detail in Chapter 5.

Social enterprise gives you an entirely new way of looking at your business. It's challenging, for sure, as you're no longer merely trying to move forward and cross a finish line marked by annual financial profit—you're now playing a holistic business game on a field of play that covers all 360 degrees.

KEY POINTS

- Social enterprises create value-added returns to a group of stakeholders beyond traditional shareholders

- Social enterprises intentionally integrate purpose, social impact, and public benefit into a business model that also creates financial profit

- Nonprofits can also be social enterprises when they adopt market-based approaches to generating earned income

- As a social enterprise, you'll be working to create positive outcomes for your workers, your community, your customers, and the environment

- New forms of corporate governance are available to protect and demonstrate a company's commitment to social enterprise

"

"It is easy to get caught in a focus on financials, but employees and customers are increasingly attracted to brands and firms that have a higher purpose. It makes a difference."

David Aaker
Vice Chairman, Prophet

CHAPTER 2
THE PURPOSE-DRIVEN MOVEMENT

Millions of conscious consumers are redefining themselves in large part by "who" they are—and this includes who they affiliate with in the world of commercial brands.

At the same time, people are increasingly hoping to find meaning in every aspect of their lives—and the good news is they want brands to participate in this discovery. Help them find it the right way, and individuals will consolidate their purchasing power with your company because they trust you to act on shared values around social and environmental issues.

This societal drive toward new identity and meaning provides two compelling reasons to start a purpose-driven company or inject purpose into an existing business.

The first is because you want to—making a lot of money isn't enough to create the sense of meaning you desire from your work. You're passionate about the challenge presented by purpose-driven enterprise and the results it can achieve. You want to know why you're getting out of bed in the morning and how to make the hard days—and there will be plenty (this is the real world, after all)—just a little bit easier.

The second reason is because you're a pragmatist, and this is pure business strategy. You recognize this change presents an opportunity to make your business more competitive. You want to gain efficiencies and create opportunities when you embrace this new way of doing business and the target audiences it affords you. Your biggest challenge will be marrying your logical instincts with the genuine approach this marketplace requires.

While most social entrepreneurs fall into the former category— I know I definitely do—either motivation is good because they both wind up creating public benefit. And that's what this is all about: using business and the profit imperative to forge positive social and environmental change.

BUILDING MEANINGFUL RELATIONSHIPS

Welcome to the world of purpose economy, where employees and consumers alike search for relationships meaningful beyond a paycheck or a purchase.

How did we arrive at this place and time, where consumers vote with dollars and employees with the investment of their time and talents?

In today's world, companies of all sizes are being asked to proactively "do good." Companies aren't being forced to this end by the government or lawyers (though there are municipalities beginning to offer incentives for this behavior, which we'll cover in Chapter 5). No, companies are being pushed to create public benefit by consumers and employees, two powerful audiences who are both exerting newfound control over businesses large and small.

Consumers now expect companies to abandon the sidelines and become proactive agents for social change, occupying a powerful role as market disrupters in the civic, nonprofit, and social/environmental arenas. Today, consumers' expectations go well beyond the purview with which traditional corporate philanthropy committees are comfortable.

Consumers have expanded the marketplace dynamic of features and benefits to public discourse, expecting companies to not only support but actually start necessary public conversations about societal problems and take stands on contentious social and environmental issues. In recent years, our business has taken high-profile public stances on gay marriage and the protection of wilderness, both charged subjects in our conservative state of Idaho. We've even taken time off work to be part of these initiatives.

The playing field is different now, folks. Companies are no longer allowed to operate like incumbents on the stump, hewing a considered, cautious, and noncontroversial approach for fearing to offend their customer base. Their public bottom line/party line toward advocating on social and environmental issues has always been milquetoast, vanilla, bland—anodyne. But that's changing.

Nowadays, the risk of not taking a stand is becoming greater than the danger of doing so. Your brand needs to demonstrate leadership and take a forceful and public position on an issue that truly matters—to your employees, to your consumers, to your supplier-partners, and to your community, whether local or global.

At the very least, if a company is not willing to take a stand and lead the charge for social change, consumers now demand that companies "do no harm." Their business products, policies, and practices must absolutely be in line with the greater social good.

Yes, the world is changing.

Three primary forces are propelling this changing dynamic in which the baton of power has been passed to the consumer:

- Digital change and individual empowerment

- Generational transformation

- Good, old-fashioned behavioral psychology

DIGITAL CHANGE AND INDIVIDUAL EMPOWERMENT

Today, consumers have more power because people are in control of the brand relationship. They've obtained this power from the liberating aspects of the digital world, newfound social influence, and a desire to self-actualize their consumption via brands that enable them to do good.

The Internet and its many technological children, from social media to crowdfunding, from consumer reviews to e-commerce and cause shopping, are enabling individuals in new ways. Consumers now have access to more information more quickly, and the power to exert influence and bypass your marketing in new ways. They also have the ability to make an individual "ask" with the expectation that your company will fulfill it. And as any opportunistic businessperson knows, you have an opportunity to deliver on it.

In short, the technology age has given individuals new power in their relationship with brands. They now routinely ask for—and receive—acts of goodness to be created on their behalf.

GENERATIONAL TRANSFORMATION

One word: Millennials (or, as one scribe puts it, the "selfie-generation"). This age group (25 to 40 years old) is redefining the marketplace. Millennials are independent spirits, from their political beliefs to their lack of trust in institutions. They are fueled in this characteristic by being the first digitally native generation—they came of age with the Internet, mobile phones, and social media, all of which enable a new singular sense of self.

This generation grew up at the speed of technology. They matured in tough economic times, which forced many of them to redefine their expectation of success. Now they define it less with material goods and more as a search for meaning in their lives, which includes—you guessed it—their relationships with brands. They expect to make even their smallest of purchases amount to something larger than the simple acquisition of a product—perhaps a donation to a cause they select. And they want to be able to trust that the companies they include in their lives are operating with a purpose beyond a financial bottom line.

You have an opportunity to build a brand consumers love. With a purpose-driven mission, you can win their brand loyalty. This sentiment runs especially deep with Millennials. Research published in *Ad Age*[1] shows 70 percent of Millennials say they always come back to the brands they love. Always.

Of course, loyalty isn't given easily. You have to earn it. And perhaps nowhere will this be more important than in the labor market, where a parallel movement toward purpose is taking place.

Research we've conducted at Oliver Russell with Millennials indicates a significant majority has a strong desire to work for companies that actively contribute to the good of society. In a group that's larger than the Baby Boomer generation and in the prime of their work lives, this will be a compelling factor to consider in your hunt for talent to power your company in the future.

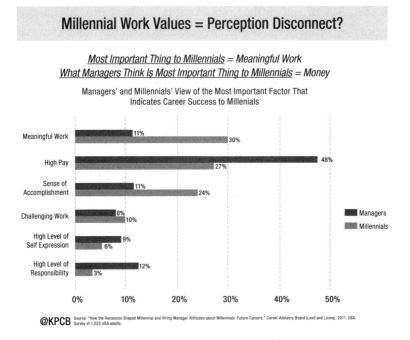

Millennial Work Values = Perception Disconnect?

Most Important Thing to Millennials = Meaningful Work
What Managers Think Is Most Important Thing to Millennials = Money

Managers' and Millennials' View of the Most Important Factor That
Indicates Career Success to Millenials

Meaningful Work — 11% / 30%
High Pay — 48% / 27%
Sense of Accomplishment — 11% / 24%
Challenging Work — 8% / 10%
High Level of Self Expression — 9% / 6%
High Level of Responsibility — 12% / 3%

Managers
Millennials

0%   10%   20%   30%   40%   50%

@KPCB Source: "How the Recession Shaped Millennial and Hiring Manager Attitudes about Millennials' Future Careers." Career Advisory Board (Levit and Licina), 2011, USA. Survey of 1,023 USA adults.

GOOD, OLD-FASHIONED BEHAVIORAL PSYCHOLOGY

So why are people so concerned with meaning now? This human drive for meaning in life stems from basic psychology. We have come to a point in our society where most of us have our basic needs met. We're talking Maslow's hierarchy of needs here.

As we work our way up through Maslow's fundamental physiological and safety building blocks, most of us have these physical needs provided, such as eating, sleeping, and a safe place to live (though clearly there are underserved segments of the population who still contend with these basic needs on a daily basis). Once we've secured these needs, we climb to the needs of love/belonging and esteem. These are the areas where companies and their brands typically enter the equation for consumers—your need to express love and tribal affiliation for a brand (say, perhaps, as a fan of the

Seattle Seahawks) or what the brand says about your status (the difference between owning a Harley-Davidson or a BMW, for instance).

We don't stop there, of course. Humans are naturally competitive and work toward satisfying ever-higher needs. Maslow believed the drive toward self-actualization was universal, whether through creative expression, the quest for truth and perfection, altruism, or other higher-level expressions. This explains the consumer's desire to form relationships with brands. We want to entrust our hard-earned dollars to companies and products that help us create meaning in our lives beyond consumption. And we want to spend our days or nights working for them, too.

This means that brands, which have long been viewed suspiciously (often rightfully so) by consumers as serving only the company's own self-interest (i.e., bottom-line profit) will be called upon to behave differently. Purpose-driven consumers will seek brands that demonstrate they care about customers beyond the transactional experience and actually share like-values. Companies will be asked to fulfill the self-interest of their consumers and even go a step further by helping customers realize their highest sense of self-worth via their experience with the brand. Companies begin this process by providing their corporate social responsibility through actions, not words, involving stakeholders in these efforts, and openly communicating both actions and results.

The bottom line: Businesses and their brands are increasingly expected to play at the top of the pyramid—to provide a service or product with fundamental features and benefits, *and* deliver an experience that helps customers and employees obtain a higher purpose.

BUILDING A CONFIDENT CORPORATE CULTURE

Social enterprise isn't just a movement of the granola crowd or dairy co-ops. In its annual Core Beliefs and Culture Study,[2] global consulting firm Deloitte says creating meaningful impact beyond financial performance is becoming a business imperative.

"If you want to be successful over the long haul, you have to have a sense of purpose that is clearly articulated and embedded in your organization and processes, but you also have to live it," said Punit Renjen, Deloitte's chairman of the board. "There can't be two sets of rules."

It's this same transparency—living the corporate values—that consumers are acutely aware of when they judge business in regard to trustworthiness. And why is that important? Simply this: In branding, dollars generally follow trust.

One of the interesting findings of Deloitte's study, now in its third year, is how purpose can positively affect company and employee confidence. If you've ever played competitive sports, you realize just how important confidence can be to success, which in this case translates into the future growth of your company.

"We wanted to see if purpose has any correlation to building business confidence," said Renjen. "We found that both short term as well as long term, there is a very tight correlation. Eighty-two percent of respondents who work for an organization with a strong sense of purpose say that they are confident that their organization will grow this year, compared to 48 percent of those who did not have a strong sense of purpose."

IGNORE THIS TREND AT YOUR OWN RISK

Social enterprise isn't a fad—it's a trend, and a powerful one at that. It's moving quickly beyond the consumer market into the business-to-business arena. In the same way geography (Buy Local, Buy American-made) or affinity (think colleges) define and drive purchasing decisions around a sense of place or tribe, businesses are starting to make purchasing decisions around socially responsible behavior and corporate values. Everything else equal, what better way for a company to support its mission than to buy from another business that shares its values?

WHAT DOES THIS MEAN FOR YOUR BUSINESS?

You have an opportunity to inject your business with a sense of meaning that resonates with your audiences and extends beyond product, paycheck, and profit. It will help you attract, retain, and motivate employees, position and differentiate your company in the minds of your customers, and open doors to new relationships with other businesses.

If your heart's not in it, this will be a tough transformation to make. Even if your heart *is* in it, it won't be easy—you will still have to be sharp, perhaps even sharper, in the way you run your business.

But I think you're up for the challenge.

KEY POINTS

- Building a social enterprise provides entrepreneurs with an opportunity to find new motivation in their work—and for some, the driving force is the distinct business opportunity it presents

- Consumers are beginning to consolidate their purchasing with companies that share their values around social and environmental issues

- Digital change and individual empowerment give people newfound power to change corporate behavior in their relationships with companies

- Generational change, led by the Millennials, is hastening this transformation in the marketplace

- Social enterprises help entrepreneurs and consumers alike fulfill "higher needs"

"

"We can still focus our energy on working for good people and good causes. It is never too late to be brave."

Margaret Wheatley
Writer and management consultant

CHAPTER 3
PURPOSE

What's your company's purpose? If your company is like most businesses, this straightforward question can be easily answered by two words: financial profit.

But not anymore. As a social entrepreneur, financial profit is an outcome of your enterprise. Your purpose is where you start. It's the primary driver of everything you do and the single most important idea you'll need to define.

Let's start by talking about purpose statements. But before we do, let's be clear about one thing; we're not talking about a mission statement here. These are outdated, as corporations have been in the business of shaping mission statements in all-day meeting retreats for a long time. Typically forged by committees, they can include everything but the kitchen sink, and are exercises in glittering generalities and corporate clichés.

Mission statements also tend to be inward facing, as a focal point for internal staff regarding the company's positioning in the marketplace—featuring its desired place in terms of products, services, or client segments. What's more, many mission statements are shaped well after the initial business has been started. It's as if someone popped their head up from the rabbit warren of gray cubicles and said, "Hey, shouldn't we have a mission statement?"

Not so with a purpose statement.

JUST ADD WHY

Your purpose is your *raison d'être*, or your reason for being. It's the answer to the "why" question—why you and your team will spend the majority of your waking hours working well beyond the paycheck. It speaks more about your place in this world and how you intend to better it—your social mission, the difference you will make in people's lives. A purpose statement imparts a sense of being rather than becoming—it's more about the *way* of work rather than a hard-and-fast ending goal.

The ultimate objective is to capture how your company will make a difference in the lives of stakeholders—far beyond a simple value proposition for your direct-paying customers.

That's the primary difference between mission and purpose—the former is self-centered and the latter is stakeholder-centric.

Think of your purpose statement as a geothermal spring that rises from the center of the earth: powerful, hot, and energetic. And everything, my friend, flows from here.

CRAFTING YOUR PURPOSE STATEMENT

As far as your place in the world, purpose will give you a sense of meaning. In crafting a statement to express your promise of commitment, you need to be succinct and motivating. The statement must be easily understood and remembered, and be compelling to your many audiences. It should be steeped in emotion. Above all, it should be simple and declarative.

Whether in the design of words or graphic elements, the notion of absence is powerful. It's more often about what doesn't appear than what does. But brevity can be tricky, and getting at the essence is tough. It takes a lot of work and time, especially when there are multiple decision-makers—co-founders, families, teams—in the mix.

In the end, what you're striving to define and express is the positive benefit you and your business want to make in the world. This is the motivating lever and the powerful "why" that draws upon basic human desires for improvement as part of a group working to achieve meaningful outcomes.

Here are a few examples of how other purpose-driven companies have approached the purpose statement:

Life Is Good
To spread the power of optimism.

Warby Parker
To offer designer eyewear at a revolutionary price, while leading the way for socially conscious businesses.

Patagonia
Build the best product, cause no unnecessary harm, use business to inspire and implement solutions to the environmental crisis.

And ours at Oliver Russell
To improve the lives of all we touch through meaningful work and the power of social enterprise.

As you can see, there's no exact formula for the right purpose statement, nor should there be. Your statement should come straight from your core, be easy to remember, and serve as differentiation for your organization.

Your goal is to inspire everyone in your company (and your stakeholders by extension) by declaring the difference your business intends to make in people's lives.

Often, a third-party facilitator with an unbiased perspective can be beneficial in helping you shape your purpose and, subsequently, your brand values. Organizational development consultants or marketing firms with experience in this area are two likely candidates to help facilitate this process. They can often guide this process through creative exercises that help to unlock your potential purpose and distill it to its essence.

Many times the best starting point for your statement is personal purpose—asking participants, such as co-founders and team members, to define their personal purpose in life and using this to spark the purpose for your social enterprise. This act of co-creation with others is powerful. Different perspectives will make your purpose statement stronger, and co-creation helps engender buy-in and engagement in working to achieve the purpose.

I also recommend involving a strong writer in the drafting process. Purpose statements should be succinct, which in its root form is the work of a smart and critical editor. Crafting a statement also gives you an opportunity to present a primary brand message to your audiences. A good writer can make your purpose statement memorable, one that's conveyed creatively, with a personality—emotion!—that makes it "stick" in the minds of your two most important stakeholders: your employees and your customers.

KEY POINTS

- While they are close relatives, a purpose statement is not a mission statement

- A purpose statement should address the positive benefits you will make externally in the lives of your stakeholders

- A well-crafted purpose statement will be a source of inspiration to your employees

- A third-party facilitator can be a great help to your team in developing a purpose statement, and a strong writer can shape a purpose statement that is succinct, creative, and memorable

"

"The real goal
of what we're
doing is to have
a positive impact
on the world."

Ed Catmull
Co-founder and President,
Pixar Animation Studios

CHAPTER 4
VALUES

While your purpose statement is the North Star toward which you navigate, your values provide the sure footing upon which you work—the "how" of your corporate foundation.

Sure, many traditional companies have business values, but their importance runs deeper when you're a values-based company with purpose as your product.

That's why a values-based business puts this code of conduct at the fore of its endeavors, in front of, or at least alongside, product and service.

Today, this often means taking action to voice and live up to your values in a very public way. In fact, Cone Communications listed this as the number one trend in CSR for 2016: companies leading with their values, demonstrating their commitment by tackling controversial topics and working to change government legislation perceived as running counter to their values.[3]

LIKE ATTRACTS LIKE
Brand values matter more than ever.

For a purpose-driven company, values act like pheromones, those chemicals emitted by insects and animals to trigger a social response in the species group. In this case, the "species" we're talking about are your customers and employees.

That's why it's so important that founders and key team members have shared values for the business as you start your company, and for the years to come. Because, like pheromones, your company's values dictate behavior; they can attract, alarm, incite, and send important signals.

Here's a story that illustrates why it's so important to establish values at the beginning.

I met with a friend recently whose business partnership, a highly successful craft brewery, was coming apart at the seams after just five years. The friction point? The partners, it turns out, did not share the same values for the way the business should be operated. They especially disagreed over the treatment of employees, a key component of a purpose-driven organization. "I really wish we'd gone through a brand-development process when we started," my friend said. "We could have aligned ourselves around shared values from the beginning and made decisions based on a common understanding."

THE VALUES-CREATION PROCESS

So how do you pick the right values? There are literally thousands of potential values to consider: creativity, teamwork, and family, to name a few. This exercise is one of collaboration among founders and key team members. It is a process of elimination, a sort of "last values standing" exercise: Which values are you most passionate about? Which values will you support and live even in the toughest of times, especially when they might cost you money?

Constructing shared values seems so simple. But it's really a vital step for founders to take. Along with developing your purpose statement, defining values can be exacting and grinding work, though your manifesto brings some music to the party, which we'll cover shortly. It's definitely not near as much fun as creating and selecting a logo.

But instead of rushing headlong into the glory work of visual identity and pithy marketing messages, it pays to take the time to create shared values. They will be a touchstone for your partnership, and provide direction for your employees and the operation of your venture well into your future. In the case of my friend, the craft brewer, agreeing to shared values up front may well have saved a partnership that ended up going south.

WHEN IT COMES TO VALUES, LESS IS MORE

I recommend distilling your core brand values to a group of three, or, at most, five. This doesn't mean ideals that don't make the cut aren't important; it just brings focus to your most important values.

Many companies select single words and leave it at that. In fact, we were guilty of that when we shaped our values 25 years ago. We now recommend framing your values with a sentence or two of supporting language for context. Unfortunately, single words by themselves can leave too much open to interpretation.

As an example, here are the values—with supporting statements—we helped a client, Rising Springs, shape for its social enterprise.

ENGAGEMENT
We value on-the-ground results driven by facts, hard work, and active participation.

PROGRESSIVE
We strive to be a force for positive change, transparent, and open to new ways of thinking.

SUSTAINABILITY
We are committed to balancing financial, social, and environmental well-being.

SIMPLICITY
We believe simplicity is the source of timeless solutions.

COMMUNITY
We take pride in the beauty and people of Idaho and seek to enhance its natural capital.

Adding context also helps ensure that you escape the values trap that snares so many companies. This happens when companies select values that are generic and meaningless—words like innovation, integrity, and excellence, which are so often interchangeably shared throughout Corporate America. These words are damaging because they have come to be viewed as disingenuous pablum. Your values should positively differentiate your company and communicate a fundamental belief system and code of conduct.

To further illustrate this idea, here's an example of a company that once upon a time was a scrappy startup, but has managed to stay true to its foundation as its three values have propelled it to success: Southwest Airlines.

1. **Warrior Spirit** (Work hard; Desire to be the best; Be courageous; Display a sense of urgency; Persevere; Innovate)

2. **Servant's Heart** (Follow the Golden Rule; Adhere to the Basic Principles; Treat others with respect; Put others first; Be egalitarian; Demonstrate proactive customer service; Embrace the SWA Family)

3. **Fun-LUVing Attitude** (Have FUN; Don't take yourself too seriously; Maintain perspective [balance]; Celebrate successes; Enjoy your work; Be a passionate Team player)

While it's missing the social mission component, we include this example as a good model for how to distill values to just three and then articulate how those values should be demonstrated.

Here's another strong example that actually comes from our hometown. The city of Boise, which has a vision to be the most livable city in the country, expresses its values through a handy brand mnemonic it created, LIV.

L - Lasting Environments. Recognize, protect, and improve the health and sustainability of all our activities, our connections to one another, and our natural resources.

I - Innovative Enterprises. Work with individuals, nonprofits, and businesses to encourage creativity and collaboration that will promote economic prosperity and improve lives.

V - Vibrant Communities. Engage citizens and organizations to spark new connections, inspire cooperation, and strengthen Boise's rich, community-minded spirit.

WHAT DO YOU STAND FOR?

"It is becoming an expectation that our companies stand for something," said Melissa Dodd, an assistant professor at the University of Central Florida who studies corporate activism, during an interview with *The Wall Street Journal.* According to research she cowrote, U.S. consumers are 8.1 percent more likely to buy from a company that shares their opinions, and 8.4 percent less likely to buy from a company that doesn't.[4]

DEFINE WHAT YOU'RE FOR—AND AGAINST

Values are about what you stand for—but an equally important aspect of your purpose-driven business is deciding what lines you won't cross (i.e., what you're against). And now, during your company's nascent stages, is the best time for this discussion.

Are there specific business practices at odds with your values that you will not condone? Are there industry segments at cross-purposes with your core operating philosophies in which you will not participate? In the socially responsible investing world, this practice has been formalized for decades via money managers using "negative" screens to determine whether or not to invest in a company. Back in the day, investments in apartheid South Africa were a no-no. These days, negative screens run the gamut from weapons to pornography to alcohol.

Now is the time to have this discussion, and not in five years' time when money's on the line. Set your fundamentals early and move forward accordingly.

If you do set your values in stone, be sure you are able to clearly articulate the definition of the category, as well as the rationale behind your decision. As with the rest of the world, there is a lot of gray here, and you need to be as clear as possible.

A CAUTIONARY TALE

As I said earlier, your values, like pheromones, can attract like-minded people to your organization. But they can also serve as an alarm that repels, so be prepared.

Here's an example. In 2015, we lost a major client because of industry segments we listed on our website as work we would not do: tobacco, petrochemicals, weapons, and pornography.

The client seemed like a great match. They had a strongly stated purpose around education and ample resources for their objectives. Indeed, the client, with its seven-figure budget, had the potential to become the largest in our agency's history.

On the eve of signing a contract, the chairman of the organization's board happened to visit our website. He took exception with our exclusion of these industry segments, as he had ownership in two weapons companies, and also did not like being categorized in the same group as pornographers. In addition, his organization's investment portfolio included petrochemical companies.

In one fell swoop, we lost the account, which was a major financial blow. I still fault myself, not for standing behind our values, but because I didn't do a good job of explaining these exclusions on our website. For instance, we're not anti-hunting, but I didn't properly explain what type of weapons we were against, such as automatic weapons for nonmilitary use.

In the end, our team at Oliver Russell was proud of our stance in the face of a big payday, but at the same time, we decided to take these exclusions off our website. We still live by these exclusions, but believe they are better used internally with deep discussions around specific instances rather than simply listed in black and white on our website. Perhaps that's just being pragmatic and not transparent, as I find myself still wondering about it. What do you think? What would you do?

GIVE YOUR VALUES SOME GROUNDING

Values can be pretty philosophical and lofty, when what they really need to be are accessible and practical. To help bring them back to Earth, we've developed a couple of measurements here at Oliver Russell.

First, we evaluate our values through a simple process.

Each year, every person at Oliver Russell reviews our performance on how we live our values. They assign a number from one to five to each value: to be creative, collaborative, progressive, and socially responsible. We're able to aggregate our rankings, average out scores, and numerically gauge how we're doing currently, and how we've improved or slipped over the past. Comments are part of the process as well, and the entire exercise provides an opportunity for open dialogue and improvement.

We also use our values as the basis for individual awards. Our team votes for individuals who have best exemplified the values over the past year. Winners are selected, publicly recognized and honored by their cohorts, and rewarded with two extra vacation days for the upcoming year.

Values are an incredible asset, your ultimate gut check. Build them into your company's foundation from the onset, then live by them, and they'll serve as a steadying influence as you navigate the inevitable cycle of business where your faith will be challenged. And, as every social entrepreneur knows, that's a powerful support system to have in place.

KEY POINTS

- Values are forever—not something to be changed to fit the fashion of the day

- Values are a fundamental code providing guidance in making everyday decisions and setting critical long-term strategy

- Don't create a set of values that runs into the double digits. This dilutes their importance and also makes it harder for your employees to remember them. Pick three to five values that are core principles

- Values have traditionally been seen as internal proof points, but are increasingly important to external stakeholders

- Values act like pheromones, attracting like-minded employees and customers

"

"An organization's culture of purpose answers the critical questions of who it is and why it exists. They have a culture of purpose beyond making a profit."

Punit Renjen
CEO, Deloitte

CHAPTER 5
CORPORATE STRUCTURE

When state legislatures, rarely in the vanguard, enact laws creating entirely new corporate legal structures to recognize a small but emerging business community, you know serious change is afoot.

That's exactly what's happening as many purpose-driven companies and organizations are pushing the government to codify their commitment to public benefit.

When you start your purpose-driven business, you'll need to select a formal legal corporate structure. Traditionally, this constituted making an election in the more common designations as a C Corporation, S Corporation, or Limited Liability Company (LLC).

ASSESSING YOUR LEGAL OPTIONS
Today, you have new options from the get-go. A number of states have adopted legislation that recognizes the new and growing class of social enterprise. The two most popular are Public Benefit Corporation and low-profit, limited liability company (L3C).

(The same opportunity is available to existing businesses with a legal designation in place. Oliver Russell was established as an

S Corporation in 1991 and added Benefit Corporation status in 2015 when it became available in the state of Idaho.)

These new classifications are often referred to as a "hybrid" corporate form, a term I don't care for—I think it creates the perception that profit and purpose are mutually exclusive, when in fact these new corporate forms acknowledge they are intertwined.

Given the legislative momentum for these types of legal designations—Benefit Corporations were first recognized in 2010 in Maryland—it's pretty much a slam dunk they will be recognized in every state at some point in the near future. As of writing this midway through 2017, 31 states and the District of Columbia have authorized Benefit Corporation legislation, and seven more are working through the process. Additionally, the state of Washington has created Social Purpose Corporation legislation, similar to that of a Benefit Corporation. California also offers both Social Purpose Corporation and Benefit Corporation options.

You don't have to select these new legal structures to operate a social enterprise, and indeed, a number of the companies we'll highlight later in the book have not taken this formal step. But I believe these legal designations offer critical protection to social enterprises, and signal a much more serious approach to your stakeholders. I have yet to hear a compelling reason from serious social entrepreneurs for not adopting legal status of these types.

I'm not an attorney, so my main objective here will be to provide a brief overview of each legal designation and let you pursue a deeper understanding with the experts.

WHAT IS BENEFIT CORPORATION STATUS?

Benefit Corporation status gives for-profit companies the flexibility to pursue social impact alongside financial results, without legal threat from investors for not maximizing shareholder value.

Keep in mind that a Benefit Corporation is not the same thing as a B Corp, which we'll discuss in the following chapter.

Legal designation as a Benefit Corporation also helps preserve your social mission as your company advances into the future with potentially different leadership and ownership.

Benefit Corporations are not a tax entity; corporations that adopt this legal designation also have a separate status for federal taxes, such as a C or S Corp.

And while the design of a Benefit Corporation gives you the flexibility to pursue these public-oriented outcomes, it also comes with a new responsibility—you will be required to demonstrate the specific public benefits you are creating.

WALKING THE WALK

Public benefit can include making a positive impact on society, workers, the community, and the environment.

As a Benefit Corporation, you'll need to publicly state your intended purpose for creating social or environmental benefit. Your operations will ultimately need to be certified by a third-party standard assessing your performance toward these aims. We'll discuss the process and choices for third-party standards, along with options for consulting assistance, in the next chapter.

A high level of transparency is required of Benefit Corporations, including the publication of an annual report detailing the public benefit you created over the past year. These can take the form of simple Word documents or PDFs that get filed with your Secretary of State, or be full-blown, four-color reports that also serve as marketing vehicles for your benefit company.

THE CASE FOR AN L3C

An L3C—a low-profit, limited liability company—is another option for social enterprises. They have a clearly stated goal of maximizing social impact—not net income. These businesses bridge the gap between nonprofits and for-profits, with the goal of generating modest profits while pursuing a business model that emphasizes socially beneficial results.

What's the appeal of an L3C? They are designed to help entrepreneurs obtain impact investment capital. L3Cs use a tranche structure that provides flexibility for different types of investors, accommodating a range from low-risk investors, such as foundations, to more aggressive venture investors. (Tranches are simply different investment segments in a company that provide varying levels of risk, reward, and maturity.)

An incentive for nonprofit foundations to invest in an L3C is that it qualifies as a Program Related Investment (PRI) for charitable purpose, which is a stipulation for maintaining a foundation's tax-exempt status.

L3Cs, much like Sub-S Corporations, also act as a pass-through for federal income tax purposes, allowing the tax liability to pass through to its members to be paid as personal income taxes.

Benefit Corporations vs. Certified B Corps

Issue	Benefit Corporations	Certified B Corporations
Accountability	Directors required to consider impact on all stakeholders	Same
Transparency	Must publish public report of overall social and environmental performance assessed against a third-party standard*	Same
Performance	Self-reported	Must achieve minimum verified score on B Impact Assessment
		Recertification required every two years against evolving standard
Availability	Available for corporations only in 30 U.S. states and D.C.**	Available to every business regardless of corporate structure, state, or country of incorporation
Cost	State filing fees from $70-$200	B Lab certification fees from $500 to $50,000/year, based on revenues
Role of B Lab	Developed Model Legislation, works for its passage and use, offers free reporting tool to meet transparency requirements; No role in oversight	Certifying body and supporting 501(c)(3), offering access to Certified B Corporation logo, portfolio of services, and vibrant community of practice among B Corps. To learn more about B Corp certification, visit www.bcorporation.net.

* Delaware benefit corps are not required to report publicly or against a third-party standard
** Oregon and Maryland offer benefit LLC options

Source: "Benefit Corporations & Certified B Corps." Benefit Corporations & Certified B Corps | Benefit Corporation. N.p., n.d. Web. 21 Dec. 2016. http://benefitcorp.net/businesses/benefit-corporations-and-certified-b-corps

While not as widespread as Benefit Corporation legislation, the L3C designation is available in a number of states.

Beyond the differences of these legal structures, there's another reason to consider formalizing your public benefit in this way: Local governments are beginning to provide incentives to these types of companies—either through tax advantages or preference in public contract procurement. Municipalities such as San Francisco and Philadelphia already have adopted this practice.

It makes sense that governments would develop ways to encourage businesses to minimize negative impact on their communities while creating positive social impact. These incentives also provide cities and regions with a stimulus for economic development by attracting these types of businesses.

WE'VE ONLY SCRATCHED THE LEGAL SURFACE

As I mentioned earlier, this is just a down-and-dirty explanation to encourage your thinking about legal designations at the formative stage of your company. Contact your Secretary of State or ask an attorney for a more detailed explanation. Your Secretary of State's office also should be able to provide you with a list of the L3Cs or Benefit Corporations in your state. See if any of them are attorneys, or simply use this as an opportunity to call the social enterprise and ask questions about the process.

A helpful, online publication that provides a deeper dive on the subject is "An Entrepreneur's Guide to Certified B Corporations and Benefit Corporations," authored by Abi Barnes and recently published (2017) by the Yale Center for Business and the Environment and Patagonia.[5]

Another good resource is the B Corporation website, which is home to a number of attorneys and legal firms well-versed in this specialized type of work.

KEY POINTS

- There is no stronger demonstration of your commitment to social enterprise than changing your company's legal status to recognize it

- Becoming a Benefit Corporation legally protects your company's mission and also requires that you demonstrate and report your public benefit

- A Benefit Corporation is not the same as a Certified B Corporation—make certain you understand the difference

- L3C designation allows for flexibility on obtaining investment capital

- Seek out social entrepreneurs and attorneys with experience in the sector as you decide what legal structure might be right for you

"

"Social entrepreneurs are not content just to give a fish or teach how to fish. They will not rest until they have revolutionized the fishing industry."

Bill Drayton
Founder and CEO, Ashoka

CHAPTER 6
PROVE IT

You've developed the philosophical foundation for your business and codified it through governance: its purpose, your values, and the organizing structure that will guide your company through the rigors of the marketplace.

You'll be working to deliver a triple bottom line, one that benefits people, the planet, and profit.

And just as a formal corporate legal structure (if you so choose) commits you to a course of public benefit, a third-party assessment of your social and environmental performance indicates that your purpose-driven enterprise is powered by deeds, not merely words.

(Even if you decide not to conduct a third-party assessment, I strongly encourage you to explore abbreviated online versions of the certification processes, as they cover subjects that will be helpful as you create your company, from workplace policies to important measures for your involvement in the community.)

BUILD LOYALTY BY BUILDING TRUST

Many of today's consumers, especially Generation Z and Millennials, are wary of corporate goodness claims. Unfortunately, talk is too often cheap in the corporate world, from decades of greenwashing to the out-and-out fraudulent. (Looking at you, Volkswagen.) Inherently transactional, superficial cause-marketing events also play a part in eroding trustworthiness, in part because of their transparent, self-motivated intentions.

The good news is that people increasingly want to form loyalty bonds with brands based upon a demonstration of a new code of corporate ethics.

They're seeking truth—even when it's not positive. As a transparent company, this is the proof you provide them, which basically is the "truth" of your company. When you proactively share the bad along with the good, you're showing them respect, and that you can be trusted.

Your number one job as an entrepreneur is to build trust. And that's exactly what certifications from credible organizations allow you to create: proof. To your people. To your customers. To your supply chain. To your community. And to yourself.

Beyond the truth, certification programs are also fantastic tools that can help your company benchmark and measure progress, while—yes—contributing to your bottom-line profitability.

DIGGING DEEPER TO THE SOURCE OF TRUTH

As a social entrepreneur, you've shouldered the harness of public benefit, and now it's time to plow the fields—and your fields are different than those of other businesses.

Let's examine the subject of community, for instance.

Traditionally, corporate community involvement has involved writing donation checks or volunteering for an annual "Paint the Town" project.

As a social enterprise, you'll dig much deeper than that. For instance, do you know how "local" your supply chain is? Keeping money flowing to local businesses is a primary economic stimulant for your community, whether purchasing lunches from a locally owned pizzeria or using an independent community bank. Staying local also minimizes environmental impact by keeping business closer to home.

Are you actively educating your suppliers to better understand your business model? Are you letting them know you make procurement decisions based upon their practices and policies?

Does your product or service benefit an underserved community such as a low-income, physically challenged, or minority group?

These are just a few of the many facets of community you'll need to consider as you build your social enterprise.

You'll go through similar in-depth exercises that examine your workplace policies, your governance, your environmental practices, and customers, among others.

B THE CHANGE: B CORPORATIONS

We've covered a lot of new territory up to this point, and you may be feeling somewhat overwhelmed. You don't have to plow these fields by yourself. There's help.

Traditional sustainability consultants don't get to the heart of purpose as they focus more on environmental inputs, outputs, and practices. Fortunately, there now are a number of methods for companies both large and small to create programs that measure and assess both environmental *and* social impact.

One increasingly popular route is to become certified as a B Corporation,[6] which is different than the Benefit Corporation status covered in the previous chapter.

Our company, Oliver Russell, is both a legal Benefit Corporation and a Certified B Corp. Why both? While Benefit Corporation designation gives us legal protections and responsibilities, the B Corp assessment process gives us the tools to measure and improve our benefit. Being part of the B Corp community also provides value beyond measurement: the support and camaraderie of kindred spirits, membership benefits and discounts, and the opportunity for collaborative partnerships among like-minded companies.

Here are just a few examples of the types of questions you can expect to be asked:

What type of employee training does your company provide for its social and environmental mission?

Are your company financials verified annually by an independent source through an audit or a review?

What percent above living wage did your lowest-paid full-time, part-time, temporary workers, and independent contractors (excluding interns) receive during the last fiscal year?

So you see, it gets at the heart of things pretty quickly, which hasn't kept more than 2,100 companies around the world, as of this writing, from becoming Certified B Corps.

The nonprofit B Lab runs this certification program and provides an online platform to walk you through an assessment of your environmental and social performance. If your company exceeds a threshold score, B Lab then certifies your company. While this is largely a self-assessment process, it has safeguards built in to help ensure the veracity of your reporting.

Certified

Corporation®

This framework also gives you a strong foundation for understanding the components of creating a purpose-driven company—what's called "measuring what matters." And once you measure what matters, you are then able to get strategic about improving your performance over time.

Using this type of assessment is an immensely valuable business tool that can result in insights that help reduce costs, boost productivity, and position your company for partnerships in the new purpose economy.

PURPOSE GETS CLOSER TO ACCOUNTING

Certification from B Lab is the best program we've found for overall assessment and measurement—my company is a Certified B Corporation[7]—but the market is quickly evolving to address the demand for programs of this nature, and there are a number of other ways for you to begin proving your purpose.

New certification platforms are being launched, such as GoodWell.[8] Its founder, Pete Gombert, is a corporate startup refugee who saw a gap in the marketplace for a certification platform designed to be simple, universal, and easy to implement.

Goodwell's certification, which is narrower than the B Corp assessment, focuses on the "people" component of a business.

GoodWell has developed a series of 11 key human metrics that provide an objective view into how an organization is behaving in regards to its employees. This gives management and boards visibility into potential problem spots. It further enables companies to demonstrate—for employees, prospective recruits, and other key stakeholders—that their intentions align with their actions.

As employers increasingly strive to retain and attract valuable talent in a competitive market—or simply get in synch with a basic societal need for companies to behave in a more humane manner—look for certifications like this to be on the rise.

Other options include big accounting and professional service firms such as Deloitte, Ernst & Young, Grant Thornton, Pricewaterhouse-Coopers, and McKinsey & Company, among others. These firms are now moving into the social-impact auditing space. However, their offerings are typically aimed toward larger, more established corporations that are coming to understand that the market is taking social impact seriously.

"There is definitely a trend for social impact reporting to become closer and closer to accounting," Jeremy Nicholls, CEO of the Social Return on Investment Network, told *The Guardian*.[9] "One of the things that is now increasingly being looked at is the interrelationship between financial reporting and social or environmental impact—or natural capital."[10]

NAVIGATING CERTIFICATION

Of course, you might not have the budget or scale required to work with a Big Four accounting firm. Fortunately, there are many other options becoming available. As the consulting world senses a business opportunity, it is quickly adapting to provide solutions for social entrepreneurs of all sizes.

One example is Ecotone Analytics GBC,[11] a specialized firm in Minneapolis that helps companies measure, manage, and communicate their social, environmental, and business impacts.

Two more credible options, each with a B Corp focus, are Conscious Brands[12] in Calgary, Alberta, and Lift Economy[13] in the San Francisco Bay area.

With any potential consultant you might hire, be a purpose-driven consumer and ask them for "proof" of their own certifications.

Of course, you can always elect to develop your own program for measurement. It's not as credible in the marketplace—after all, you're the one doing the measurement—and you'll miss out on the community aspect of a certification platform. But perhaps you're at a different starting point and that's what works for you right now.

Additionally, there are other tools to help you identify metrics considered to be important. Three that are worth a look are the GRI (Global Reporting Initiative)[14] for sustainability reporting; IRIS,[15] an initiative of the Global Impact Investing Network;[16] and UN Sustainable Development Goals.[17]

VERTICAL INDUSTRY CERTIFICATIONS

You may also be interested in other less holistic ways to prove your performance, which can be compelling to employees and consumers, and also provide important components to your overall social impact measurement.

You can work on your supply chain verification through industry associations relevant to your company. For instance, Europe's Fairwear Foundation,[18] an organization comprised of 120 brands, works to verify and improve labor conditions for garment workers.

You can become a member of 1% for the Planet[19] and join an alliance of businesses financially committed to creating a healthy planet. Other highly regarded certification systems which may be valuable for you to consider include the Rainforest Alliance, Fair Trade Certified, LEED for building performance, FSC from the Forestry Stewardship Council, and EnergyStar.

And if you're looking to raise capital, you can obtain certification through various programs such as GIIRS[20] (Global Impact Investing Rating System, also spawned by B Lab) that enable impact investors to better assess your company.

There are many, many worthwhile programs like these that can be of great help to you. The certifications these organizations provide are stamps of security for various audiences and can buttress your credentials. Keep in mind, however, they should serve to augment, not substitute for, a complete and ongoing third-party certification of your company.

THIS SOUNDS LIKE A LOT OF WORK

Social enterprise involves serious programs that require work and commitment. But social entrepreneurs are a serious breed, too—you aren't looking for a rubber stamp, you're looking for a permanent tattoo.

They do require work. And they do cost money. But I can promise you, they are worth it.

Our designation as a B Corporation requires that we recertify every two years. This requires approximately 50 to 60 hours of time. (While the first certification is the most rigorous, each subsequent effort will take less time, as you'll have the baselines in place and an overall better understanding of the process.)

When Oliver Russell first certified, we paid an annual fee of $500. As we've grown in size, we now pay $1,000 each year for our certification and the support services provided to this community of social enterprises.

Beyond certification, you'll also need to invest operational time and money on an ongoing basis to assess, compare, and improve your social and environmental performance.

So yes, there's an investment, and it's not inconsequential. But if you think about it, the return you get from your investment is profoundly consequential: the truth.

KEY POINTS

- Certification is the basis for creating trust with your stakeholders, as it provides "proof" of your actions from independent, third-party groups

- Certification also provides a valuable framework to help you measure and improve your operations and your ability to deliver social and environmental impact

- There are many different certification systems ranging from complete corporate performance, such as Certified B Corporation, to vertical, industry-specific certifications, such as the Rainbow Alliance, the Forestry Stewardship Council, and Fair Trade Certified

- There are numerous consultants who specialize in a broader definition of sustainability (environmental, social, and financial) that can benefit your company whether you formally certify or not

"

"I'm encouraging young people to become social business entrepreneurs and contribute to the world, rather than just making money. Making money is no fun. Contributing to and changing the world is a lot more fun."

Muhammad Yunus
Nobel Peace Prize winner and founder,
Grameen Bank

CHAPTER 7
PEOPLE

Where we seem to be doing things most differently at Oliver Russell is in the area of people, particularly with our workforce. But before we get into that, let's talk about a broadened definition around "people."

Of course, the first place to start when considering the idea of people is with your employees.

Rather than platitudes—think, "People are our most valuable asset"—a purpose-driven company regards employees as its most critical resource, one to be nurtured and sustained rather than exhausted and played out like a mine with a short-term life expectancy.

Perhaps what's most important here is to change your view from top-down. Instead of thinking of your team as "your employees," think of them as your coworkers, fellow human beings who are committed to professional success and also have wants and needs that can be mutually fulfilled by a purposeful workplace.

CREATIVE BENEFITS, HAPPY PEOPLE

At Oliver Russell, we provide a few interesting benefits to the people on our team. We have a healthy-living benefit where every person receives $50 a month to purchase a product or service that will make them healthier. That could be a YMCA membership, acupuncture, or a new baby carrier for a bicycle.

Healthier people are not only happier; they're also more productive and create less demand on our health care system. Plus, that type of health benefit is a creative way to say the company appreciates the individual and values their overall health.

We also provide a stipend for alternative transportation. If one of our team members walks to work, rides their bike, takes public transportation, or carpools, they receive the cash equivalent of a day's paid parking. It's not much, but it does add up and also helps diminish the environmental impact of traffic.

These are all attractive benefits, but I think the most important part of recognizing a person's worth in the workplace is by making an investment in work-life balance.

Our company, Oliver Russell, has measured its performance on work-life balance yearly since 1997. In the nearly 20 years we've surveyed our team, the results consistently show this is the most important issue to our workforce—even routinely outpolling compensation.

ADVANCING WORK-LIFE BALANCE

Here are a few ways we try to advance work-life balance at our company.

All of these ideas revolve around treatment of employees, which I argely centers on policies and implementation practices.

We allow team members to work flexible hours that fit their lifestyles. It turns out most people work around the same schedule, though some come in early and some arrive later. But everyone has the ability to come and go throughout the day as they please.

We have the ability to work remotely at Oliver Russell. If you want to keep good people, you need to extend the boundaries of your office. We have team members who work from home while juggling childcare. We've had people move away for a spouse's schooling and work for us from a college campus several states away. We have some who work from other remote locations, be that their living room or a coffee shop, because they find those environments help them be more productive.

Does this provide challenges? Sure. When you're not in the office you don't benefit from the social lubricant of working in physical proximity to the team. Not being around sometimes means you miss out on ideas and discussions that happen on an impromptu basis. However, the most important thing for making the remote situation work is effective communication. And as anyone who's ever sent an email to a coworker sitting several feet away can attest, there are challenges to effective communication within office walls as well.

Lastly, we try to work reasonable hours. We don't believe that working 12-hour days on end is a badge of courage. We frankly don't think it's smart or sustainable, so we discourage it. That doesn't mean there aren't occasions to work longer and harder, but when it becomes the rule rather than the exception, it's symptomatic of a longer-term problem with your organization.

MORE UNEXPECTED WORK-LIFE BENEFITS

Coming down with a cold? Oliver Russell has an unlimited sick leave policy—if an employee is sick, they can just stay at home and forego the cost/benefit calculation of subtracting a personal leave or vacation day from their yearly allotment. This helps people recuperate faster, and when they don't come to the office, they can't expose coworkers to germs.

Here's been one of the most interesting things about our sick leave policy. We've had the same policy for about 10 years, and as best I can tell, as both a businessperson and a student of human nature, it's never been abused.

What to expect while you're expecting at Oliver Russell? We try to make things easier for new parents. While, as a business of fewer than 50 employees, we aren't required to comply with the Family Medical Leave Act, we provide maternity leave. Paid. And we provide paternity leave. Also paid. Talk about a time where people value (and need) work-life balance!

We also created a benefit for employees to receive paid time off to volunteer in the community. We try to model this civic spirit of engagement in our business through an active volunteer program, and we aim to stimulate this in our coworkers' lives outside of work with a benefit that matches personal volunteer time with paid time off.

ONE SIZE DOESN'T FIT ALL

I realize this way of doing business can be viewed as challenging, and especially so for different types of businesses. After all, manufacturing machines can't run without operators (excepting, of course, robotics), and customers can't shop at retailers without the help of salespeople. Every business is different and can creatively shape the ways it engenders work-life balance. My point is, if you intend to create a purpose-driven workplace, your number one priority should be creating work-life balance for the people who are its economic engine.

Now, this doesn't mean you can't have high expectations for your coworkers. On the contrary, you can and should have high expectations for your coworkers, as they likely have high expectations for their company; the combination of the two is a powerful force.

This is by no means an exhaustive list—or even the right list of benefits for your business. Instead, it is intended to provide examples of ways you can invest in the work-life balance of your people.

The Oliver Russell team volunteers locally for fantastic nonprofits like the Ronald McDonald House—and as far away as the Dominican Republic.

Again, the B Corporation certification from B Lab provides useful guidance for practices and policies that are considered critical to a sustainable workplace. Indeed, one of our proudest achievements is that our company, Oliver Russell, has now been named as being Best for the World for Workers[21] among the B Corporation community for two consecutive years, and here in our home state we've also been recognized as one of the Best Places to Work in Idaho.[22]

KEY POINTS

- You can't be a successful purpose-driven business without a purpose-driven workplace

- Treating workers well makes it easier to recruit new talent and retain your experienced employees, saving costs and increasing productivity

- Work-life balance is perhaps the most valuable benefit you can provide to your workers

- A custom creative approach can provide benefits in your workplace that are high value but don't necessarily cost a lot

"

"We can no longer define success as just greater profits. That's obviously important (no margin, no mission) but true success leads to a stronger and healthier community and environment as well."

Jay Coen Gilbert
Co-founder, B Lab

CHAPTER 8
FUNDING YOUR SOCIAL ENTERPRISE

When I started Oliver Russell, I funded it through traditional means. I hustled for new clients and got them to pay a portion of their bill with cash up front, if possible. Then I aggressively managed my receivables—calling a client the minute an invoice was due for payment, sometimes even a couple of days prior. I'd simultaneously stretch my supplier payments to their maximum terms (and then some). I'd augment cash flow at pressure points through the miracle of plastic, a.k.a. my personal Visa card, which certainly isn't the lowest cost of capital but does the trick in a jiffy. In fact, my credit card remained part of the mix for a long time, eventually to be replaced by an operating line of credit from a bank.

A few years ago, I co-founded a social enterprise startup, Social Good Network, which was an entirely different beast. My co-founder and I built this on a dream to turn online purchases into donations for nonprofits. We wanted to scale the idea rapidly, which required outside investment capital.

We first went the "friends and family" route, which is exactly what it sounds like—pitch your friends and your family on either loaning you money or taking an equity stake in your fledgling venture. We obtained capital from those close to us in the form of convertible debt—in essence, they loaned us money, which accrued interest over a set period of time, and were then able to convert this debt into company equity at a future date and for a discounted price. It's not an unusual route for social entrepreneurs to use. Let's face it—often the only people who will assume the risk of your venture, combined with your desire to create public benefit, are those who know and love you.

Next, we expanded our horizons to solicit investments from angel investors. We successfully acquired investments from two regional groups of organized angels, in addition to a number of individual investors. All in all, we raised more than $500,000 in seed capital from investors who believed in our dream.

All the while, we continued to acquire new customers and work on our product, pivoting here and there as the market responded to our offering in ways we didn't foresee, and as new competition entered the fray. And we continued fundraising, always, always, always fundraising, meeting with individuals far from our home base in Boise, attending conferences in Utah and New York City, meeting with venture capitalists in Silicon Valley, and pretty much going wherever an investor with means would be willing to hear our story.

We gave it a good run, but in the end we had to close Social Good Network because we weren't successful in raising additional rounds of capital.

In the few short years since, the world of impact investing has rapidly evolved and become more favorable for social entrepreneurs. There are any number of funding avenues available to you as an early-stage social entrepreneur.

INDIVIDUALS

Beyond friends and family, there is one group that genuinely cares about what you're doing, and that's other social entrepreneurs who have been there, done that, or might still be doing it.

Generally, this is the best place to start when seeking funding. Plus, other social entrepreneurs have experience that's especially relevant to you. I believe they're also more open and welcoming to your entreaties, and they care more about what you're doing than other investors.

Here's how I'd go about doing it. I'd determine which social ventures in my community have been backed by individuals and I'd seek out those investors. After all, the hallmark of successful early-stage investment is diversification so these people will likely welcome the introduction to your company. I'd expand this to other social enterprises via a web search; often a startup's investors comprise their advisory or corporate boards, and I'd begin trying to make connections and target from there.

I'd also research the powerhouse nonprofits and foundations in my area and try to learn more about their boards—individuals who serve on them are often chosen for the three W's: work, wealth, and wisdom. They're also predisposed to community service, interested in causes, and have demonstrated they're willing to invest their own time in seeking positive change. For these reasons, there's probably a potential investor or two sneaking around in these organizations.

INCUBATORS AND ACCELERATORS

While incubators and accelerators might not offer investment capital—indeed, you often pay for the opportunity to be involved in either—they provide a critical conduit toward acquiring capital.

They're great places to intensively work on improving your social enterprise, and they provide powerful opportunities for networking with investors.

There are quite a few of these opportunities found across North America. The Spring Activator[23] in Vancouver, British Columbia, is part of a networked global startup school for entrepreneurs who want to build a better world. Here in the United States, Hub Ventures[24] in San Francisco, GoodCompany Ventures[25] in Philadelphia, UNLTD USA[26] in Austin, and the Unreasonable Institute[27] in Boulder are just a few examples.

Even the powerful Y Combinator[28] and TechStars[29] accelerators are recognizing the movement and increasing participation by social ventures for their startup ecosystem. In fact, 50 percent of TechStar's 2016 cohort in Boston was comprised of mission-driven startups.

INVESTOR GROUPS AND NETWORKS

Some investor groups not only specialize in, but also seek out investments in social enterprises. These groups aggregate investor funds and provide opportunity for individual members to participate in curated deals. Here are several to get you started:

Investors' Circle connects its network of angels, venture capitalists, foundations, and family offices with social enterprises that solve social and environmental challenges.[30]

Enable Impact is an online marketplace that helps accredited investors find profitable returns and purpose through impact investing.[31]

Toniic is a global financial ecosystem comprised of family offices, individuals, foundations, and funds looking to make impact investments that promote a just and sustainable economy.[32]

Even AngelList, a longtime player in the world of online startup capital, now provides access to investors interested in social entrepreneurship startups.[33]

If you're considering these groups for funding, it's advantageous to obtain a GIIRS rating. GIIRS, which stands for Global Impact Investing Ratings System, assesses your company's social and environmental impact and is a key analytics tool used by serious impact investors.

VENTURE CAPITAL

Over the past several years, VCs have, as they say, "woke" to the opportunity created by mission-driven startups that deliver financial returns by solving a social or environmental problem. That's good news if and when you ever get to the stage of acquiring VC investment.

If you do, you'll find there's a wide range of VCs investing in the space, from those more closely aligned to social enterprise, like Kapor Capital,[34] the venture capital arm of the Kapor Center for Social Impact, to VCs that don't focus on social enterprise but won't turn their nose up at a great investment deal, such as heavyweight Andreessen Horowitz.[35] A recent example of a new VC firm launched specifically to find return at the confluence of purpose and profit is Aera VC.[36] You can even find niche venture investors such as the Force For Good Fund,[37] which invests in women and people of color-owned B Corps, and Stray Dog Capital,[38] which funds alternatives to the use of animals in the supply chain. You can see there's something for everyone here.

The Kapor Center actually represents a hybrid model for an impact investment firm, one that makes both grants and equity investments. The Omidiyar Network,[39] which pioneered this approach, and the Chan Zuckerberg Initiative[40] are two other high-profile examples of this.

PRIVATE FOUNDATIONS

One of the more exciting fundraising developments for social enterprises comes from the world of private foundations, those sleepy monolithic bastions of wealth that disbursed grants to the nonprofits of your parents' generation.

Well, they aren't so sleepy anymore. In addition to providing grant support to nonprofits, foundations are beginning to make investments in for-profit social enterprises.

Foundations make these investments through a PRI, or program-related investment. PRIs enable private foundations to pursue their mission and meet their mandated distribution program requirements. Generally 5 percent of a foundation's investment assets are distributed annually as grants, with some portion of this also comprising PRIs in the form of a loan, a loan guarantee, or actually purchasing stock in a for-profit organization that helps further the foundation's charter.

Another investment vehicle available to foundations for social venture investment is an MRI, or mission-related investment. An MRI differs from a PRI in that it comes from the endowment— the other 95 percent beyond the 5 percent stipulated for programs. Indeed, as I write this, the powerful Ford Foundation just announced it will allocate up to $1 billion of its endowment to MRIs over the next 10 years.[41]

While PRIs have been around a long time, the IRS issued guidance in 2016 to encourage their use. Seeing as how private foundations make annual grant distributions that rival venture capital investments—in 2015, charitable foundations provided grants totaling $50 billion, while venture capital investments registered $59 billion[42]—this has the potential to seriously and positively affect the flow of capital to social entrepreneurs.

BANKS

Okay, so banks probably won't be investing in your social enterprise any time soon, but they can provide valuable financial resources in the form of operating lines of credit.

You should find a bank with a stated mission that revolves around public benefit. These institutions might come with a certification, such as banks that are B Corporations, or they might be independent community banks[43] and credit unions that reinvest in your local community.

Even if you don't require debt financing, you should seek out relationships with these types of banks, even if only for a business checking account. When you empower a relationship with another organization with a social mission, like a bank, you multiply the use of your funds for good.

Here are several banks and other institutions that provide social enterprises with loans or credit:

The Beneficial State Bank,[44] New Resource Bank,[45] and Spring Bank[46] are all examples of Certified B Corporation financial institutes. In some form or another, they all pursue access to financial services for underserved communities, relationships that contribute to the planet's sustainability, and lending to socially and environmentally responsible businesses. Sunrise Banks[47] is another B Corp bank that offers business services while providing financial products and assistance to distressed communities and underserved markets.

RSF Social Finance[48] isn't a bank. It doesn't provide business checking accounts, and its purview also includes the nonprofit world. It does, however, make loans to for-profit businesses that have a social mission at their core. They also make very small ($500 to $3,500) seed grants to organizations in social finance, food and agriculture, education, the arts, and ecological stewardship.

CROWDFUNDING

Over the years, I've learned enough about crowdfunding to be dangerous. I'm a fan of fewer rather than more investors for social enterprise startups, so I'll stay away from the type of crowdfunding-for-equity occasioned by the JOBS act.

Here's what you should use crowdfunding for: launching a product or service to test its appeal in the marketplace, creating proven revenue (which potential investors will love), and providing critical cash flow for your operations.

One social enterprise startup I've gotten to know, ReGrained,[49] used this approach to raise more than $30,000 in an initial crowdfunding campaign. They introduced consumers to their product, healthy snack bars made from spent beer grains used in the craft-brewing process, and acquired valuable bridge capital to their next funding round.

PARTNERS AND PRIVATE COMPANIES

Ah, now it's time to think creatively. Certainly you have suppliers. Would they be interested in making an investment in the future of their customer (your company)? If you're a business-to-business player and a supplier yourself, perhaps your customer might want to invest in your opportunity? Maybe it's even another supplier with whom you don't compete, but with whom you share a distribution channel, who would be an interested investor.

Explore all the concentric circles of your business. Perhaps your customers or suppliers aren't interested in investing in your social enterprise, but you never know—a discussion about investing could turn into an agreement for better payment terms, a discount on purchasing, or even a referral to a new customer.

Here's another idea that's close to home: Find a branding agency that specializes in startups and pitch them on an investment. My company, Oliver Russell, makes investments in social enterprises, sometimes through a mixture of in-kind services and cash for equity. I know others in our industry segment do this as well. So be sure to include this in your many rounds of "asks" to potential investors and supplier partners.

This is actually a new trend—successful social enterprises making intentional investments in startups as a way to support the sector, diversify assets, and hopefully, just hopefully, make a sound return as well. You can read more about the rise in companies becoming impact investors in Chapter 12.

LESSONS

Instead of providing key points at the end of this chapter, I'll share a few lessons from my experience raising capital as a social entrepreneur.

- Don't rush into investor capital. Be lean and take as long as possible with your product and team. Acquiring investment capital is a full-time job. It's exhausting. And once you've obtained it, the job of communicating with your shareholders begins. And then the next round of fundraising commences. Pitch decks, iterations, phone calls, travel. The hunt for investors takes away from Job Number One—working to get traction (and revenue) in the marketplace. When the time is right, just be sure you and your company are ready for it.

- Not all investors are alike—and you shouldn't necessarily take every check that comes through the door. You need to find those who are aligned with your mission, and I also like investors who have had their own startup experience. Beyond that, it's helpful if they have experience in your industry, a skill set (finance, marketing), or powerful connections. If you think you might pursue venture capital at some point, it's also wise to consult a pro as you consider the terms and types of early-stage investments in your company. These could affect your ability to acquire venture capital at a later date.

- When you do bring outside investors to the party, you'll need to develop a strong and highly attuned sense for which advice to act upon and which to bypass. Even then, you'll have more advice proffered by your investors than you have time for, and it's always a balancing act to be respectful of their opinions. Be strong and focused and don't try to make everyone happy. In the end, I wish I'd done a better job of this at Social Good Network.

- If you have limited resources and are thinking about certifying as a B Corporation (or other certification), put it off until your venture has a strong foundation. We certified Social Good Network as a B Corporation. It quickly gained recognition as "Best Overall For the World" among the B Corp community, but that didn't really mean much when we failed. While it wasn't onerous, that time would have been better spent elsewhere.

- A note of caution on using family and friends as investors. These are still family and friends, so if your venture goes south, you will have to confront some ugly realities with them. I still remember some of the calls and tough discussions when I let mine know we had lost their investment—not fun and considerably different than with the angel investors, who have a lot of experience with this.

- Finally, a note about self-funding your social venture. I used a number of mechanisms to help Social Good Network get off the ground in the early days. I even withdrew a significant amount of money from my personal retirement account to help initially fund Social Good Network and then to keep it running when trouble came. It wasn't that I didn't realize I was putting my funds at risk. I did. I had the bug. I just believed we would be successful, and if the money went away, it went away. But what I hadn't quite thought through was the impact on my taxes.

When you withdraw money from your tax-deferred retirement fund, it's treated as income in the year you withdraw it. Conceptually, I noted that and filed it away someplace. But in the whirlwind of trying to keep a struggling venture afloat, I somehow forgot. So I got hit with the double whammy of closing Social Good Network in the same year I was hit with a significant tax bill based on six figures of income that were withdrawn from my retirement plan and ultimately lost. I basically had to pay the government for the privilege of losing money. Ouch. That wasn't very smart, and I'd recommend a "hands-off" approach for entrepreneurs with their retirement plans—especially to older entrepreneurs who are in their 50s like me.

"

"We can't leave it up to politicians; even good ones need support from business leaders to drive change."

Richard Branson
Founder, Virgin Group

CHAPTER 9
SHARING YOUR STORY

Now that you've built the foundation of your company around purpose, you're ready to launch (or relaunch) your business.

Do you have a story worth sharing? Hell yes!

This is where it gets interesting. When you work with purpose, you work with intent. You're creating a story driven by pride and meaning. Your story, I've found, becomes much easier to tell and, frankly, sell.

That's because while every business has a story to tell, your message is different than most. It's not just about a product with new, improved packaging or a time-saving function. You're sharing a captivating story; what David Aaker, the godfather of modern branding, calls a higher-purpose brand.

A big side benefit of building a socially conscious business is that you're creating a brand that is real, a brand that is human. And that's what people are trying to find.

CELEBRATE WHAT MAKES YOU DIFFERENT

You have a brand value proposition that's a key differentiator in the competitive marketplace—so use it!

And right now, our growing class of companies is different enough that people find these stories refreshing and respond to them favorably. Most people are naturally attracted to companies with a higher purpose.

After all, we live in a world where Hollywood enshrines characters such as Gordon Gekko, who proclaims, "Greed is good!" and where a rapaciously profitable, real-world investment bank CEO declares, "I'm doing God's work." Considering these role models and the challenges we face on our planet, who doesn't want the good guys in business to win? And congratulations, you're one of those good guys.

Our company, Oliver Russell, earns its stock in trade by helping build brands for purpose-driven companies. We have a lot of experience in telling socially responsible stories.

So when I thought about writing this book—and specifically including this chapter—someone said to me, "You're giving away the gold," as in, "That's what companies pay you for." Well, yes, that's true, but one of the hallmarks of this purpose-driven movement is its open-source nature. The way I look at it, if our company's purpose is *"to improve the lives of all we touch through meaningful work and the power of social enterprise,"* well, the more we share, the more we live our own mission by propelling purpose in the marketplace.

You've got a unique storytelling opportunity, too. And the more successful you are in sharing it, the more you improve your chances of thriving as a social enterprise. That means you'll help solve more social and environmental problems around the world in the process.

STARTER IDEAS FOR INTERNAL COMMUNICATIONS

To help make the most of communicating that higher purpose of yours, let's first focus on your primary target audience.

Most companies overlook their number one constituency: their employees. This is where you should always begin as a purpose-driven venture.

It's likely that your employees are already looped into the process you've just navigated, at least to varying degrees. But let's perform a quick reality check here. While you've been working diligently to create a purpose-driven company, your employees have been occupied by the demands of their day-to-day jobs. So now it's incumbent on you to get them up to speed, facilitate buy-in, and motivate them.

You've already provided leadership up to this point; now it's time to appoint a champion among your employees who will help direct purposeful engagement in your company. Having another co-worker champion this effort will facilitate ownership of the idea and implementation by gaining buy-in via cohorts, rather than being burdened by the appearance of a top-down approach.

This person can lead weekly (or monthly) brown bags to educate your team on the many aspects of purpose. Group settings like these offer an excellent opportunity for team building as well. Don't forget, this is an occasion for employee engagement and a big-bang return on the investment you've made in the process. Your company offers people a chance to find meaning through their work; don't overlook the opportunity to reinforce it with your workers.

HOW TO REACH YOUR TEAM

So how do you reach your team? It's not necessarily an easy task or every company would be doing a better job of engaging its employees—but you do have a built-in network and communications tools already at your disposal. Here are just a few ideas to get you started.

- Webinars and Podcasts. For companies with multiple locations or larger workforces, webinars and podcasts are excellent ways to foster understanding. A side benefit to these options is that they can be repurposed to work for external audiences as well.

- Engagement Around Values. Ask your employees to memorize your values. If you've limited the number of values to a core group of three, or even five, this shouldn't be too tough. Spot-test people in meetings and reward correct answers, even in a small way. You might even make a commitment to begin regular staff meetings with a discussion about your values— what they mean to people, how they're playing out in reality, how they factor into day-to-day decisions—or answer questions that have come up.

- Fly Your Certification Flag. If you've received a certification from an independent verification body, use this symbol on your business cards and consider adding your purpose statement to the card as well. Do the same for the signature line of all company email accounts.

- Hash It Out on Social Media. Provide your employees with a #hashtag and sample messages, in case they want to use their personal networks to share your purpose.

- Tap Others' Toolkits. If you've worked with an independent certification authority in the process, or even with a consultant, they may also have tools and tactics you can use in communicating your purpose to employees.

THE MANIFESTO

One of the best tools we've found for capturing the imagination of your purpose and values is a manifesto, so let's spend some time with that here.

Your manifesto is typically a motivating proclamation of your purpose—you can turn it into a workplace poster, offer it as a PDF, or even use it as the creative theme for a video. While I believe its principal application is a rallying cry for employees, your manifesto increasingly serves double duty as a powerful public declaration to external constituencies who seek to align their values around businesses they support.

Be sure to hire a strong creative writer to help. The more powerful manifestos take the form of what could be a compelling oratory.

Here are some examples to give you an idea of what I'm talking about.

SIMPLE

A SUSTAINABLE SHOE MANUFACTURER

Less > More.

Houston, we've got a problem.

Bigger, better, and faster have taken the wheel. And spun us out of control. We've been melting glaciers, banishing bee colonies, and devolving the human race into a rat race.

It's Gimme Gimme Gimme.

When is enough, enough?

Would it really kill us to trade down for once?

Let's tweak the definition of wealth.
And accumulate some good karma.

It's time to get greedy for the stuff that really matters.

We're taking a stand against
The shenanigans of excess.

It's time for
More give than take
More good than bad
More positive than negative.

We propose a recalculation of the fuzzy math.
A simple equation to help play in an age where less > more.

Keep it real.
Keep it simple.

(RED)

A RETAIL BRANDING AND LICENSING INITIATIVE FIGHTING AIDS

Every generation is known for something. Let's be the one to deliver an AIDS FREE GENERATION.

We all have tremendous power. What we choose to do or even buy, can affect someone's life on the other side of the world.

In 2002, more than 1,500 babies were born every day with HIV. Today that number is just over 600. We must act now to get that close to zero.

(RED) can't accomplish this alone. It will take all of us to get there—governments, health organizations, companies, and you.

When you DO THE (RED) THING, a (RED) partner will give up some of its profits to fight AIDS.

It's as simple as that.

BE (RED). Start the end of AIDS now.

SWEETGREEN
A FAST-FOOD CHAIN FEATURING HEALTHY FOODS
Your time is now. Work on purpose and with purpose.
Make real friends. Share inspirations.
Never get stuck. Challenge yourself.
Beware the status quo. Enhance your communities.
Leave a gentle footprint. Be a contribution today.
Savor everyday moments and gifts.
Keep it real. Create the change you desire.
Climb higher. Find beauty in simplicity.
Pursue your passions.

There are many other ways to accomplish employee engagement around your purpose. The basic idea is to leave no stone unturned in communicating your purpose to employees first, and continually thereafter, for its ultimate success rests on their shoulders and in their voices and their hearts.

After all, they're your best sales team.

SHARING YOUR STORY WITH BROADER STAKEHOLDERS

Along your journey, you'll need to share your purpose with other audiences. Customers are a no-brainer, so let's first consider groups that might not seem so obvious.

SUPPLIERS

Your suppliers are a key constituency. Why? You'll want them to understand this vital aspect of your business so they can work with you better. Your supply chain is a critical part of your purpose, not only because it can help spread your message, but because you can spark powerful change here as well. By educating suppliers about your purpose, you take the first step toward converting the business partners in your supply chain to seek maximum impact by using their businesses as a force for good. Just because you're the one signing the check doesn't mean you should overlook this key audience.

LOCAL GOVERNMENT AND CIVIC ORGANIZATIONS

Make certain your city, county, and chamber of commerce, among others, are aware of your purpose. Sharing this information with them will help shift perspectives in the business community toward a "different" type of business. You might even be able to advocate, as is being done in some places, for preferential treatment on public contracts for businesses that have adopted and demonstrated an intentional commitment to sustainable operations.

If there are communities built around a certifying process, such as B Corporations, don't forget to market to this community as well.

While we're on this topic, one way to share your purpose is to simply give preference to partnerships and relationships with businesses that share your values. After all, if you want to further business as a force for good, you should buy from other businesses sharing your values and goals.

There is a quid pro quo to this—other companies will search you out for this very same reason. I see this happening right now in our business—companies intentionally seeking and purchasing from us because we share and act upon similar values. We'll highlight a few examples in the next chapter.

PURPOSE—THE FIFTH "P" IN THE MARKETING EQUATION

Rubber hits the road with your customers. Research indicates that the tribe of purpose-driven consumers is large and in charge, and gaining traction by the day. This scale is causing companies to consider "purpose" along with the rest of the traditional P's in the marketing equation: price, place, product, and promotion.

Here are some steps for sharing your purpose externally, both as a mechanism to spread the message, and to promote and differentiate your products, services, and your company brand and business model.

FIND YOUR VOICE

First, a brief word about voice. Your brand should have its own original brand personality, one that differentiates you and hopefully makes you appealing to your target audience. However, it's critical to remember that when you tell your story of purpose, you don't have to shout. In fact, you shouldn't. Actions speak louder than words, which is ultimately how you'll create a confident company that resonates with purpose-driven consumers. You'll discover that people will hitch their wagons to yours and willingly share your story for you. All of which is just another valuable reason for bringing purpose into your business.

THE SUN IN YOUR PURPOSE SOLAR SYSTEM

Your website should be the sun at the center of your galaxy. All information about your purpose should reside here, not only for visitors but also as a content marketing distribution mechanism for sharing—and expanding—your sphere of influence on social media and through email marketing.

WRITE, REWRITE, THEN WRITE SOME MORE

Writing begins by actively blogging about your purpose in your editorial mix alongside products, services, and other topics. (You are blogging, aren't you?) The original content you generate positions you as a thought leader, makes you smarter about the subject, is a great place for employee education, and provides baseline content for posting on other social media channels.

PUBLISH AN ANNUAL REPORT

While you're writing, why not write an annual report? If you're a legal Benefit Corporation, this is a requirement. Either way, it's a great idea to produce one voluntarily because it's an exceptionally effective and accepted format for telling your overall success narrative over a period of time.

Virtually every stakeholder group you have, from employees to suppliers to customers, will be interested in your annual report. The format can be as creative as you choose. It should tell your story and, just like traditional financial annual reports, it should communicate your numbers—the measurable social impact you've achieved, the lives you've affected, the seeds you've sown. It also affords you a valuable publicity opportunity by crafting a news release highlighting your yearly results and alerting the news media to the report's availability.

Our Oliver Russell annual benefit report.

DIGITAL MARKETING

Email is an effective way to disseminate your purpose as well. Be sure to deliver your annual report, and any other thought leadership on the subject, as part of your regular email content to customers.

This blog content can be customized and promoted on social media as part of your regular editorial mix. To carry your message even more broadly to social influencers interested in this topic, use some of the more popular social impact hashtags: #socent, #socinn, #socimp, and #impinv.

You should also participate in relevant social media discussion groups that would be interested in your news—and from which you would likely benefit by joining. As an example, LinkedIn has forums for discussing social entrepreneurship[50] and cause marketing.[51]

EARN IT WITH PR

While you didn't add purpose to your business just for the PR, it creates an excellent opportunity to receive exposure in the media—in your home community for sure—but with a little effort, the opportunity extends far beyond your local news.

Two good choices for reaching the right media and influencers with your news and thought leadership are CSRwire[52] and TriplePundit.[53] CSRwire (CSR standing for corporate social responsibility) works more like a traditional newswire, carrying your news to editors and reporters, as well as to online influencers. TriplePundit is a social media machine (as well as a Certified B Corporation) that provides exposure to a business community that cares about sustainability and purpose. While both charge for content distribution, they each offer incredible exposure and reach for your business, driving traffic to your website and providing valuable links to boost website search engine optimization (SEO).

You can also garner publicity through free press release services such as PR Log.[54] Note that these free services don't have focused, built-in media lists covering the purpose economy. They will, however, get your news out while providing some SEO benefits. Understand the operative word here is "free," and you get what you pay for.

Also, be sure to distribute your news releases about purpose to your industry's trade publications. They'll likely be interested in this news angle as an emerging trend, and it can position you as a leader in your industry.

Additionally, there are other players in the media, especially digital, that can provide a platform for your news. You can easily identify and pitch other media who routinely cover this segment of the economy, such as the *Huffington Post*'s Purpose+Profit[55] and Forbes' Social Entrepreneurship.[56] And there are many, many bloggers covering the category who may be interested in your story as well. Just start by appending "socially responsible," "social impact," or other descriptors to the subject of "bloggers," and an entire universe of influencers will reveal itself to you.

THE WORLD BEYOND THIS STARTER KIT

This starter kit is certainly not meant to be all-encompassing. My intent is to encourage you to share your story of purpose with others in ways that can ignite employee engagement, accelerate the overall movement, and provide your company with a promotional boost that differentiates you from the competition. If you're trying to maximize your social impact, why not use it to your advantage?

KEY POINTS

- The world is looking for brands that are real, that are human. A receptive audience awaits your story as a social enterprise

- Use your purpose as an advantage—the more successful you are, the better off the world is

- Start by sharing your story inside the company with your team so they are on board, feel valued, and can become your most effective storytellers

- Focus your external efforts on digital storytelling, social media, and PR

- Two communications tools not to be overlooked: a manifesto serving as a rallying cry for your purpose and an annual report detailing specifics of the social impact you have created

"

"As a side note,
I was really
impressed with
your business
orientation as
a public benefit
corporation. Keep
up the great work."

Oliver Russell
New Business Prospect,
March 2017

CHAPTER 10
THE BUSINESS CASE FOR PURPOSE

I'd like to interrupt this feel-good message with a brief chapter I hope will dissuade you from thinking this is purely a Kumbaya-singing, Birkenstock-wearing, tie-dyed movement.

Don't get me wrong, we're all in business and money's still the primary fuel that makes the marketplace go round. We have to recognize this—and, as one sage social entrepreneur told me—"No margin, no mission." After all, if financial profit weren't important to your model, you'd be starting a nonprofit.

Because, social enterprise truly is all about the business—and there are cold, hard, pragmatic benefits to this approach. I'll share just a few of them with you here.

In Chapter 2, I told you there were two reasons to start a purpose-driven company.

The first was to satisfy an ingrained need for creating meaning in your life and public benefit beyond your immediate business.

The second was more of an MBA case study: to seize a burgeoning business opportunity.

Personally, over my career I could have definitely made more money, but it wouldn't have made a difference. That's always been my driver—making a difference—so I fall squarely in the first category.

I have no doubt that you can be every bit as profitable as a regular business, whether driven by passion or pragmatism. I've just chosen to invest a larger portion of our company's profits in the community, which is where I get my deepest return.

The choice is yours.

Let's look at a few primary business benefits through the prism of the purpose-driven movement's holy trinity of people, planet, and profit. It's an apt, alliterative mnemonic, with individual components interrelated and, in some ways, sequential: How you create the "p" in financial profit is largely an outcome of the investments you make in people and planet.

COMPANIES WITH SHARED VALUES ARE MAGNETIC

We've talked about how purpose can provide new opportunities with a new and growing class of consumers looking to align their purchasing with businesses that share their values. This will likely result in a more efficient customer acquisition and retention strategy.

What's often overlooked, however, is the same attraction occurring in the business-to-business (B2B) market. Businesses looking to maximize their social impact are trading with other businesses that share the same goal.

These companies aren't choosing you because they're simply enamored with your values and looking for an emotional high. It's much more pragmatic than that. If you're trying to make social and environmental change, it's only smart—all else being equal—that you spend your money with others who are trying to make similar change. That's the way a socioeconomic movement gathers momentum.

This claim isn't theoretical, but earned from our experience at Oliver Russell. I can tell you that over the past year we've had numerous companies approach us about working together—specifically because our values (social and environmental) align with theirs.

These aren't your traditional companies. They're all purpose-driven startups, and if you think they're helmed by Millennials, you'd be wrong—I'd guess the median age of these company founders is 45 and up.

And none of them are in Idaho, where we're based, so they actively had to search us out. We're now working with like-minded entrepreneurs who hail from New Orleans, California, and Singapore, and we're all maximizing our impact by spending with one another.

VETTING THE SUPPLY CHAIN

What I've described above with B2B is an informal entrepreneurial method for vetting your supply chain. And it's happening at larger corporations as well.

To illustrate my point, here's another anecdote from our experience at Oliver Russell. We recently went through a process to re-qualify for work as a roster agency with a longtime Fortune 50 customer. The usual process, which includes a qualitative work review, financial benchmarks, and a thousand other metrics, included a new twist this go-round.

For the first time in our long relationship, we were asked to document and substantiate our operational commitments and measurable progress toward positive social and environmental practices. As a company that has long committed to measuring its practices in this area, we were only too happy to comply.

The examples I've shared so far are both about creating new business opportunities and minimizing marketing expenses. There are many other ways you can save money by being a purpose-driven business.

BOOSTING ENVIRONMENTAL SAVINGS

A key area for savings involves your purpose-driven business's environmental impact. Among others, you'll measure inputs (such as energy and raw materials) and outputs (think waste), and you'll analyze your practices surrounding the use of resources.

The idea is to minimize your environmental footprint while you operate as a business.

The benefit, aside from the environmental good, is that when you conserve resources, you also conserve cash. This provides possibly the easiest tangible metric to understand the financial benefit of becoming a purpose-driven organization. For example, if you lower your bill from the power company, you put that savings straight to the bottom line.

Our business tries to follow best practices here, but we don't do anything revolutionary. We monitor energy consumption and set reduction targets. The more we reduce these inputs, the more we help conserve resources for the planet and for our profit-and-loss statement.

Conserving resources isn't rocket science. This past winter at Oliver Russell we turned down our thermostat several degrees. We bought everyone Patagonia jacket sweaters, which kept people warm and made them happy. We paid off this investment during the first season, and subsequent savings—running into the hundreds of dollars each month—accrue straight to our bottom line.

How do you turn down the thermostat and still beat winter?
You buy your employees Patagonia sweater jackets.

GOING GREEN SAVES YOU GREEN

Additionally, we research different ways to create environmental savings, such as our internally infamous "waterless urinal" project, which didn't make the cut because we're in a region with low-cost water, and the return on investment for the urinals turned out to be decades long.

As a social entrepreneur, you'll also help shape environmental policies, such as minimizing business travel to reduce fuel consumption. While this doesn't replace direct human contact, especially when building new relationships, we're moving toward teleconferencing whenever possible. You'd be surprised how quickly thousands of dollars in savings can add up when you aren't spending them on airfare, hotels, rental cars, and restaurants. Oh, and then there's that significant environmental benefit you create as well. Bonus.

ENHANCING YOUR RECRUITMENT EFFORTS

I speak from experience when I say that having a higher purpose serves as a powerful recruiting tool for hiring the best available talent.

I have, on average, about one person a day approach me, usually via email, about working at Oliver Russell. It usually goes something like this: "I'm inspired by the company you're building and want to work there." It's never a garden-variety inquiry about an available position, but rather expresses that Oliver Russell is the type of company they want to work for (and, by the way, when a job opens up, I'd love to be considered).

What's surprising to me is the caliber and range of these prospects— from honors-bearing, newly graduated college students to accomplished professionals at the tops of their careers, all wanting to work at a small company in Boise. (For that matter, they probably think it's Boise, Iowa, instead of Idaho—what's important to them isn't location, it's purpose.)

Here we have those pheromones at work again—your purpose attracts others with similar interests, and in this case it reduces your recruitment costs significantly. I haven't had to pay for a job listing in years because I have a large file of qualified candidates who have expressed a strong desire to work for Oliver Russell. We're in the great position of having our choice of the best candidates.

IMPROVE EMPLOYEE RETENTION

How much does it cost to hire and train someone? What's the cost of going without a key person for several weeks or months?

You don't have to answer those rhetorical questions. But I can almost see you squirming in your seat as you consider them, because you know just like I do that losing key people is an expensive proposition.

Purpose is an incredibly powerful tool in the workplace. Once people have a taste of it, they want more—and if a competing job offer doesn't provide it, this lack of purpose presents a barrier to departure. Purpose is certainly not insurmountable, but it's formidable. We've had just one person leave our company through their own choice over the past several years, and that was solely because the competing offer included a 50 percent pay increase.

A DIFFERENT DEFINITION OF PROFIT

So you can see how this philosophy, put into practice, then flows into profit, which really is an amalgam of the three P's: The way you run your business will create financial profit for you and your shareholders, while also delivering public benefit to your many stakeholders.

Truth be told, I think this for-profit, purpose-driven orientation is actually more challenging than others. But I also think the rigor and discipline it requires makes you a better businessperson and provides the opportunity for sustainable, long-term financial profit going forward.

You just have to be up for the challenge, willing to evolve, and embrace a different definition of profit.

KEY POINTS

- A socially conscious business is conservative in practice, creating cost savings through improved environmental performance

- This way of doing business mandates a new level of operational discipline and efficiency

- Both customer and employee acquisition and retention can be made more effective

- You now have a key marketing differentiator that successfully attracts new business opportunities

"

"A little bit of good can turn into a whole lot of good when fueled by the commitment of a social entrepreneur."

Jeffrey Skoll
Founder and Chairman,
Skoll Foundation

CHAPTER 11
SUCCESS STORIES

I've spent most of this book sharing my ideas for how to build a purpose-driven company. But what's really exciting to me is seeing the ways other social entrepreneurs put these principles into action.

You're probably aware of highly publicized examples such as Patagonia, TOMS shoes, and Warby Parker. They're all for-profit companies that have developed innovative products and businesses aimed at fostering social and environmental change.

For sure, they are leaders and models for the rest of us, but I think it's even more instructive, and perhaps equally important, to look at companies that are just as creative and socially-minded, but not as well-known.

Some of these companies are just getting off the ground, while others have proven their business models over a decade of experience. They're all led by talented businesspeople and have creative approaches to providing value in the marketplace. And while not all of them have taken the step to undergo a certification process or legally incorporate their benefit, they all have inspiring purposes at the heart of their endeavors.

ASPIRATION

An investment firm with a social conscience? Get out of here!

Well, consider this: Aspiration is a social enterprise and investment firm with a mission to help customers make money *and* make a difference at the same time.

Aspiration is a different cat. Designed as an investment vehicle that serves the middle class, its team uses an online platform and an inclusive philosophy about investment strategies that have traditionally been limited to only the wealthiest investors.

While most of the financial services industry is normally staid, this brash startup doesn't hide its intentions. It recently posted a tweet saying, "The goal is to do to Wall Street investment houses what Uber is doing to the taxi industry."

Aspiration makes its services accessible to nearly any investor, as you can start by investing as little as $100. (I initially invested $500.) And here's another kicker—you get to choose the fee you pay for their services, from nothing up to 2 percent. (I've chosen 2 percent because this is the kind of behavior I want to encourage in an investment partner.)

Aspiration also embraces a spirit of giving by donating 10 percent of its revenue—get that, *revenue*, not profit—to microloans for struggling Americans. (That's another reason I selected the higher fee of 2 percent, because it maximizes my part in Aspiration's giving.) These loans help people living at or below the poverty line start their own small businesses.

Aspiration also makes it easy for customers to embrace the spirit of giving by providing a donation platform on its website. Through Aspiration, customers can make donations to nonprofits that work together as part of six nonprofit "mutual funds" committed to solving complicated global issues.

Aspiration is quickly collecting its share of fans, customers, and accolades, too—this year it was named to *Fast Company*'s list of the World's 50 Most Innovative Companies, also ranking at #3 for Social Good and #4 in Finance.

I said earlier in the book that the world of for-profit social impact is attracting a lot of seasoned people, and Aspiration CEO Andrei Cherny is a good example. He's been co-founder and president of a media startup, worked in the White House, served in the Naval Reserve, and prosecuted financial fraud. Oh, he's also an author and a historian, too.

BOLL & BRANCH

A husband and wife decide to go shopping for a new set of sheets in New Jersey. They're inquisitive—she's a third-grade teacher, he's a tech entrepreneur—so they ask lots of questions: Why do some sheets sell for $500 and others far less? How and where were the sheets made? Who made them?

A response with shrugged shoulders was the norm, as salespeople couldn't answer what Missy and Scott Tannen thought were pretty basic questions. It got them thinking: Was the price spread an opportunity to disrupt the marketplace? And what about those questions of provenance—was there a story to be created and told by a company who could answer these questions?

And that's how a third-grade teacher and a techie got into the business of selling bed sheets—and in the process became reformers for a supply chain known for its unethical practices.

Missy and Scott started Boll & Branch in 2014. Their idea was to make high-quality, organic bedding, go direct to the consumer at a greatly reduced price, and develop 100-percent certainty and transparency throughout the supply chain.

If you're a guy like me, you generally go slack-jawed when you finally discover how much quality bedding costs. Missy and Scott's disruptive direct model offers high-quality sheets (I've bought and can vouch; my wife sings their praises) at about half the price of similar quality sheets. That's a big win, right?

Well, what's even more cool is their purpose: They work to deliver better products based on solid ethics—the couple set out to change an industry (textiles) known for its unfair—and even inhumane—practices.

Boll & Branch directly sources its sheets in India, from cotton that's grown in extremely poor areas of the country. Boll & Branch knows where each product is manufactured and the farm where the cotton is grown, including the parcel and even the farmer's name.

The bedding company also became the first in the world to be Fair Trade Certified. And Fair Trade-established prices enable farmers to earn 15 to 20 percent higher prices for their cotton. Also, because many farmers have switched to growing organic cotton to meet Boll & Branch's specifications, they're no longer exposed to dangerous chemicals. As they don't have to pay for these chemicals, their profits are further increased, another benefit.

Boll & Branch's ethical approach extends to the mills as well, where workers weaving sheets receive fair wages and medical insurance, and work only eight-hour days, among other standards.

The company also has a partnership with the nonprofit Not For Sale, contributing funds that have helped support nearly 10,000 victims rescued from human trafficking.

Boll & Branch has since added towels, knit blankets, scarves, and other products, and has grown explosively, which is no great surprise. After all, what's not to love about the company? You'll save big on great bedding and, if you're like me, you'll appreciate a business approach that lets you sleep a little better at night.

EVERYTABLE

Here's another feel-good story that started on Wall Street, before it migrated its way west to the City of Angels.

Sam Polk made a lot of money as a trader on Wall Street, but was alternately disillusioned by the ethics of the finance industry and motivated to find a new direction with a sense of personal purpose. He started life anew in Los Angeles and created Groceryships, an educational nonprofit providing nutrition counseling, cooking classes, fresh produce, and support groups for family food providers in the low-income neighborhoods of South Los Angeles.

It was here he met his Everytable co-founder, David Foster, who volunteered at Groceryships.

Through their intimate experience of working one-on-one with family food providers, the two came to realize that one of the biggest obstacles facing healthy eating in food deserts—urban areas where it's hard to purchase affordable, healthy food—came down to simple convenience. After a long day of work, what hardworking parents in low-income neighborhoods really needed were healthy, ready-to-go meals priced affordably.

Now, generally you can easily find food with two of those three qualities, as traditional fast-food providers are only too happy to provide meals that are ready-to-go and priced affordably. But how to deliver on the promise of "healthy"? Well, that's the real trick.

And leave it to two guys from the high-finance world to figure out this problem might just be solved by a variable-pricing model.

Thus Everytable was born, a public benefit corporation with a mission to make good food available to everyone.

When you eat at Everytable, you're paying less and bringing better food to more communities. Here's how it works: Everytable prices its meals according to the neighborhoods it serves. Its variable-pricing model is an innovative spin on buy one, give one—meals in low-income neighborhoods cost $4, which is just above break even, while the same meals at Everytable in high-income areas cost $8.

The company's plan calls to always open its grab-and-go stores in tandem, an outlet in a low-income neighborhood for every store it opens in a high-income area. In summer 2016, it launched in South Los Angeles, where per-capita income is $13,000, as well as in downtown LA, where income is much higher. The Everytable price downtown is competitive with other healthy fast-food outlets there, and serves to support the company's ability to provide lower-cost meals at its South LA store. This story is proactively communicated to customers at the point-of-sale.

Everytable uses a hub-and-spoke distribution model to help keep costs down. It prepares meals in a central commissary, which eliminates the need for on-site kitchens. This reduces the size of its retail footprint, saving on both lease and labor costs (no kitchens, no cooks).

Inspired by the local community's traditional cuisine, the meals are made from scratch each day. All healthy, all tasty, we're told—with meals ranging from Vietnamese Chicken Salad to Pozole Rojo, and Jamaican Jerk Chicken to Cajun Blackened Fish.

The restaurant biz is tough, as is the world of startups, but I think Sam and David might just be on to something with their idea. I know I'd eat there because I believe in the mission and, like everyone else, I'm time pressed as well. We'll see how successful they'll become, but I'm really pulling for Everytable and everything they bring to the—pardon the pun—table.

HEADFRAME SPIRITS AND RED ANTS PANTS

I couldn't decide which of two Montana companies I wanted to profile, so what the heck—I'll tell you about both of them. These intriguing businesses in the Big Sky State prove social enterprise isn't the province of the coasts and big cities, but can also take flight in places like Butte and White Sulphur Springs, Montana.

These two companies, Headframe Spirits and Red Ants Pants, are led by women entrepreneurs with a "get 'er done" attitude. And perhaps that's apt in a state like Montana, which was at the forefront of the women's suffrage movement in the early 20th century, and elected the country's first congresswoman, Jeanette Rankin. (It presages a larger change in corporate leadership, but more about that in the next chapter.)

HEADFRAME SPIRITS

Can you use a business to catalyze a community? That's what Courtney McKee and her husband, John, are trying to find out.

Headframe Spirits is the story of a mid-career pivot, a historic mining town, and a love for community building.

The McKees started the company in 2010 in Butte, Montana (or as the locals say, Butte, America). John's a local boy—graduated from Montana Tech in town. His previous employer, a startup that was working to produce biofuels, had just gone belly-up and left him without a job—not an unusual circumstance in this historic mining town that's seen its share of economic ups and downs.

Fortunately, his former job also left him with an expertise—how to distill fats, grease, and vegetable oil into biofuel—and Courtney now saw an opportunity to put John's experience to bear on a product with an evergreen demand—booze.

And that's how the two of them came to start Headframe Spirits, a distillery that makes, among others, Neversweat Whiskey, Anselmo Gin, and their high-selling bourbon cream liquor, Orphan Girl, all named after Butte's colorful and historic mines. These products are now available in 21 states.

Courtney serves as CEO and John serves as chief technology officer for Headframe Spirits, which also has a thriving consulting and manufacturing business that creates custom, continuous-flow distillation systems for other spirits producers.

It's a great entrepreneurial bootstraps story of pivoting around the cards that were dealt. But what's really interesting about Head-frame Spirits is the broader purpose around which it rallies: using its business to build community through civic spirit and revitalizing economic development through Made-in-America manufacturing.

"From the business side, we're really vocal about our role in our community," says Courtney. "We're not here to succeed *in* our community; we're here to succeed *for* our community. We take all opportunities to give back—financially, through our time, our resources, our voice, our employees, and ourselves."

To understand the Headframe story, it helps to know a bit about Butte. At the end of the 19th century, Butte was one of the most prosperous cities in the country. Its mines provided a key element, copper, that was in great demand with the advent of electricity. (The name Headframe pays homage to the large, timber structures that were used to lower miners into the earth and haul them back up—along with the ore they had mined.)

By the 1980s, however, most of the mines were closed and Butte, like many mining towns, has been economically challenged ever since.

Headframe Spirits celebrates this heritage while serving to spark an optimistic path toward future economic growth. The founders launched the company with a powerful give-back philosophy in the community, and they've contributed more than $200,000 over the past four years to area nonprofits.

Courtney and John are taking the first steps toward their vision of remediating an old mining yard that will be home to an expanded manufacturing and distilling operation. When completed, it will make Headframe Spirits the largest distillery west of the Mississippi. That'll create 50 to 100 new, technology-based manufacturing jobs in a town that sorely needs them.

It's here, as well, where the founders envision revitalizing a part of Butte's mining history by adding a future tourism component that will attract new dollars into the community.

As if that wasn't enough, Courtney is in the process of starting a nonprofit, Butte Innovates, whose sole mission is to spur economic development for the area.

The McKees could likely make their expansion happen more quickly, but they're eschewing outside investment capital to keep ownership in Butte. They also plan to continue building community from the inside out, by transitioning ownership of the company and making it employee-owned in the near future.

Montana took stock of their efforts in 2013 by naming them the state's Entrepreneurs of the Year, and the McKees formalized their commitment to socially conscious business by certifying Headframe Spirits as a B Corporation in early 2016.

"I make booze for a living, and I spin it into community," says Courtney. "How could it get better than that?"

RED ANTS PANTS

Okay, so for starters, how can you not fall in love with a company that calls itself "Red Ants Pants"? I'll just have to file it under the category of companies I wished I'd named here at Oliver Russell.

Sarah Calhoun started Red Ants Pants in White Sulphur Springs, Montana (population 970-ish) in 2006, and her story starts like that of many entrepreneurs—finding a gap in the marketplace.

Calhoun grew up on a farm and worked for years leading trail crews and teaching for Outward Bound. She was trying to find workwear that fit her, but couldn't—because most work pants worn by women are tailored for men; women just have to make do because there aren't any other options.

"I needed a damn pair of pants that fit!" she said. "And none of the companies I talked to told me they would make workwear for women, so I made my own."

And folks, the pants she makes aren't just any old pants—they're rugged, get-your-hands-dirty, build-up-some-calluses, break-a-sweat work pants—designed for women who fit that bill.

(Or as the company proudly proclaims on its website, "We know butts, we know curves, and we know hips. In fact, we celebrate them.")

Calhoun designed Red Ants Pants especially for women, with a straight version that accommodates narrower hips and a wider waist, and a curvy cut for women who need a little more room in the seat and thighs. (The company now also makes shorts, t-shirts, and aprons, among other products.)

The company, which promotes a 100-percent Made-in-America ethic, celebrates hard work and the value of personal, human connection. It lives by a mission statement that resonates with employers, customers, and the community alike:

Our Mission:
We provide women's workwear
for the makers and the growers,
for the builders and the doers.
We support them with humor & heart,
quality & class,
integrity & courage.
Always.

And while Red Ants Pants's rugged products are cut especially for women, they're also designed with a higher purpose beyond working in the fields and welding shops. That purpose is to help promote the nonprofit Red Ants Pants Foundation, which Calhoun started to foster strength and self-reliance in women, and in rural, agricultural communities.

The foundation's mission is to expand leadership roles for women, support working family farms and ranches, and enrich rural communities.

It accomplishes this work through a novel funding mechanism. Calhoun decided to fuel the foundation with fun, launching the Red Ants Pants Music Festival, an annual celebration that features country music and promotes rural culture. (No small potatoes here—festival headliners have included Merle Haggard, Emmylou Harris, and Charley Pride.) The festival's net proceeds are funneled to the foundation, which in turn awards community grants to recipients with similar missions.

Calhoun's another example of the quality of person who's plunged into the world of social enterprise. She's been invited to the White House for a forum on jobs and economic development. She's served as a U.S. delegate to the APEC (Asia-Pacific Economic Cooperation) Women in Business Summit. And, like the McKees at Headframe Spirits, she's also been recognized as a Montana Entrepreneur of the Year.

"Supporting women's leadership, working family farms and ranches, and rural communities is what I get excited about," says Calhoun. "I want to share that excitement and support others who are involved with similar initiatives."

From Andrei through Sarah, it's an inspiring group of kick-ass social entrepreneurs who are using ingenuity, moxie, business acumen—and purpose—to build successful companies delivering social impact. These are just a few of the role models blazing a path for others to follow. So what's keeping you? What's *your* purpose?

KEY POINTS

- Social entrepreneurs are at work in nearly every sector of the economy, from re-imagining the financial services industry to re-engineering a more equitable food system

- Certifying your company or becoming a legal Benefit Corporation is a best practice

- It's not a requirement to certify your business or become a legal Benefit Corporation to be a social enterprise—but you do need to have a purpose and values that align with measurably making a difference in the world

- Social enterprises aren't just the province of large metropolitan areas—you can find them prospering in small towns as well

- At the heart of every social enterprise is a smart, passionate human being who is committing their career to being a changemaker

"

"What business entrepreneurs are to the economy, social entrepreneurs are to social change. They are the driven, creative individuals who question the status quo, exploit new opportunities, refuse to give up, and remake the world for the better."

David Bornstein
Journalist

CHAPTER 12
THE ROAD AHEAD

Is the incorporation of purpose real or simply de riguer, fashionable, a flash among the softest of hearts in a marketplace that demands the coldest and most calculating of competitors?

As you probably suspect, I believe the purpose-driven movement represents a fundamental shift in the way we conduct business. It encompasses both the warmth of heart as well as the pragmatic calculation required to succeed in business.

While we're in the movement's formative stages, I'm convinced the integration of purpose into enterprise will gather momentum and critical mass in several years' time. Perhaps it will even come to rival previous economic transformations of the past hundred years, the Industrial and Information Ages.

That's a pretty sweeping statement, so I'll offer six specific predictions for the future that buttress my overall premise.

CERTIFICATIONS BECOME STANDARD OPERATING EQUIPMENT

I think the biggest change we'll see in the coming years revolves around certification, our enhanced technological ability for measurement and analytics, and how these assessments and ratings systems are used throughout society.

While niche today, in 10 years' time the majority of corporations will hold certifications, complete with levels or numerical rankings within the designation, for their social, environmental, and financial performance. The driving source for this change, however, might surprise you.

I don't believe consumers will drive this change—it's too tough to aggregate such a highly fragmented audience. This change will occur through the self-policing actions of businesses themselves. I believe companies will embrace certification to manage risk in their supply chains, which will have a cascading effect through the power of procurement policies.

Large corporations have been here before, primarily in terms of environmental audits, and are already pursuing broadened social standards throughout their supply chain. Why? It's in their interest to be as clean and risk-free in their supply chain as possible. Companies such as Nike and Walmart (yes, Walmart!) are already imposing social requirements on their suppliers (think child labor), and Hewlett-Packard, our own longtime client at Oliver Russell, recently included social sustainability in our biyearly review. The power of procurement will be the stick that compels many businesses to pursue certification. And that's a good thing.

THE INTEGRATED REPORT TAKES CENTER STAGE

In 2014, the European Union (EU) mandated that companies meeting certain criteria, including number of personnel and total net value, among others, must include information on their sustainability measures in their annual reports. This information includes "policies, risks, and results" related to "social, environmental, and human-rights impact, diversity, and anti-corruption policies." The measure formally went into effect at the tail end of 2016, and companies must begin reporting on these measures in 2018, covering the 2017-2018 financial year. It's estimated that approximately 6,000 companies across the EU will fall under the new guidelines.

Don't expect mandatory sustainability reporting to be an EU exclusive for long. What began for some as a "nice to have" has now become an essential communication vehicle for companies and organizations worldwide. Amidst initial hand-wringing and fears of too much transparency, the corporate sustainability report is on track to replace (or more likely integrate with) the traditional annual report. This is a good thing. Smart businesses will get out in front of this trend and not wait until it becomes mandatory. This means putting the people and measurement tools in place now.

Pick up most any annual report and you'll find eight to ten pages of preamble before you get to the real meat and purpose—Form 10-K. Much like a cigarette is a vehicle to deliver nicotine, the annual report is a 10-K delivery system. Corporate writers and/or outside agencies spend countless hours drafting and designing them, and investor relations emissaries carry them to and fro in the hopes of luring new money. Too often these reports fall flat on investors, and that's a shame.

Many companies are now finding they can make a case for combining the annual and sustainability reports. This type of "integrated report" likely will become much more common—if not the norm—in the years to come. For Wall Street, sustainability reporting has become an expectation, and it's not going away. Of note, this includes new reporting mandates from the U.S. Securities and Exchange Commission addressing material risks including climate change impacts and CEO pay multiples relative to median employee pay.

For investors, an integrated report makes sense in that it provides an all-in-one, holistic view of the company. And from a company perspective, an integrated report presents an opportunity for time and resource savings, and for enhanced business optimization.

RATING SYSTEMS PROLIFERATE ACROSS ALL WALKS OF LIFE

We've got a thirst, and a newfound digital ability, for measuring actions beyond stated intention. But don't assume the purpose revolution will be limited to companies—it won't, as constituencies ranging from individuals to city governments will be motivated by a key question: How do we score higher?

Let's start with individuals. I can clearly see the evolution of a rating system born in the purpose movement that's adapted for consumers. Think of it like this: As a consumer, you will be rated on a number of fronts, from your energy usage to your charitable donations, from your volunteer hours and social advocacy to the purchases you make from certified companies. You'll receive a number based upon these actions, which will be fluid and gamified by companies to serve multiple purposes: stroke your ego, encourage measurable improvement of sustainable actions, and provide behavior-based rewards such as discounts and special offers. I can even see your "number" being used as an employment screen or to align values and actions with prospective dating opportunities.

Cities will filter certifications to minimize impacts to infrastructure, promote community building, and limit consumption of precious resources. They will reward certified businesses and higher-performing companies with preferential vendor treatment and tax advantages. Conceptually, they might also use these metrics to target potential companies as part of economic development efforts.

In the same vein, cities will also be judged, as these certifications and ratings can be extended more broadly as proxies for quality of life. In other words, a professional in Boston looking to move to Bend, Oregon, or Boise, Idaho, might weigh a city's rankings in the decision-making process. The federal government might also use this information in their formulas for allocating funding to local governments.

And in all of the examples above, it will be highly advantageous to improve your score. Lines will increasingly blur among companies, nonprofits, and governments, with business increasingly picking up the slack.

DISRUPTION HELPS A NEW BREED OF NONPROFITS FLOURISH

This convergence of cultures will cause a disruption that will bring pain and contraction to the nonprofit sector.

As part of their mission, purpose-driven companies engage in work creating positive environmental and social outcomes. Typically, these projects have been the province of nonprofits, but I see more of this happening in self-directed efforts by companies ranging from independent volunteer initiatives to impact investing. (I also see foundations becoming more actively involved and bypassing non-profits by pursuing their own projects, and individuals doing the same via crowdfunding and crowdworking initiatives.)

The same thing will likely happen in the public sector. Municipalities, counties, and states—all the way up to the federal government—are confronting escalating problems and needs for services and infrastructure with the handcuffs of constrained funding. Who will step in to solve these problems? Progressive companies, well-versed in the triple-bottom-line model of business, will take the extra step to pursue independent initiatives that solve problems, create societal benefit, and deliver profit. People will not only accept this, they'll begin expecting it.

In the nonprofit world, this way of doing business will introduce a new competitive element, or perhaps we'll look at it as "coopetition," where nonprofits long accustomed to working cooperatively with companies will actually be competing with them to provide social services. This coopetition potentially reduces funding, volunteers, and project opportunities as well. I have to think our universe of nonprofits, currently at about 1.5 million in the United States, will surely contract.

The good news? Nonprofits are a critical part of our country's fabric, and this disruption will make surviving organizations far stronger than they are today. They'll be less reliant on contributed income via donations and foundation grants, and more adept at generating earned income via services and products—becoming yet another social enterprise operating with a model for public benefit. This business model shift in revenue could become especially important if the federal government continues to explore expanding tax revenues by eliminating the charitable deduction.

My prediction here is, admittedly, pretty much based on gut feel. After all, there's only so much money to go around. But what if social enterprise actually helps grow the overall giving pie, rather than just slicing the existing funding pie into smaller pieces? Now wouldn't that be great?

COMPANIES BECOME IMPACT INVESTORS

I'm seeing progress toward a tipping point where purpose-driven companies aren't merely limiting themselves to their own efforts for public benefit. Instead, they're pursuing a new breed of corporate activism by investing in startups that promise to do the same.

We all know how the pendulum of money works. It's powerful and swings both ways. Right now, it's swinging the right way—up, up, up, as a force for good. Looking at the big picture, socially responsible investing accounts for more than $6 trillion. But what's most interesting to me are the ways small and mid-size corporations make direct impact investments.

Companies like Patagonia, TOMS, and even our business, Oliver Russell, are now making impact investments outside their core businesses, taking equity stakes in other social enterprises that can deliver social, environmental, and financial returns on invested capital.

Patagonia Works

Patagonia Works, the holding company for the outdoor apparel and gear company, has created "$20 Million and Change," an investment fund that makes impact investments in startup companies working to bring about positive benefits for the environment. (The initial capital contributed to the fund was $20 million, thus the name.)

So far, Patagonia Works has invested in eight social enterprises that include the following:

- California Cropwise, a startup that makes liquid fertilizer from unsold food it collects from grocery stores

- Yerdle, a sharing website that keeps products in circulation and out of the waste stream

- An innovative new clean energy investment with Kina'ole Capital, New Resource Bank, Beneficial State Bank, and Sungevity (all B Corporations) to create a $35 million tax equity fund to help homeowners purchase rooftop solar power systems

TOMS Social Entrepreneurship Fund

Shoe seller TOMS has created the TOMS Social Entrepreneurship Fund to invest in the next generation of entrepreneurs using business to improve lives. So far it has invested in 12 portfolio companies, including Thrive Market, a website that sells and delivers healthy foods and natural products; Rubicon, a company that helps businesses save on waste and recycling; and Everytable, the startup profiled in Chapter 11.

Keep in mind that neither Patagonia nor TOMS has abandoned its traditional giving programs or partnerships; these equity investments represent an opportunity to strengthen both companies beyond charitable giving. They extend the reach of their brands, incubate new ideas and collaborations, and diversify business risk beyond their core industries and product lines.

Meanwhile, at Oliver Russell we're operating on a slightly different scale. We're making our first equity investment in a social enterprise, Works Progress Administration[57] (WPA), a craft brewer that will create "progress through beer," operating under a business model committed to public benefit. We intend to identify one investment opportunity per year, which will expand our impact and diversify our business at the same time. (Of course, you could also make the argument that, just like Warren Buffett, we're simply investing in what we know.)

WORKERS AND WOMEN WILL RISE IN A PURPOSE-DRIVEN ECONOMY

I believe this shift in the way we approach the role of business will significantly increase the influence of two groups: workers and women.

Let's first cover workers.

I believe we'll see a return to a concept that's been around since medieval times—guilds, in this case where large groups of people will associate around commerce for mutual benefit.

I doubt they'll be called guilds, an archaic-sounding term—but perhaps as two somewhat fringe ideas whose acronyms you'll probably recognize: Co-ops and ESOPs.

(Just so we're all on the same page, a quick turn to the Merriam-Webster dictionary says Co-ops are a business or organization owned and operated by the people who work there; ESOPs are Employee Stock Ownership Programs used as instruments for employees to obtain equity in their companies.)

In an economy increasingly moving toward independent contractors and freelancers, worker-owned co-ops and employee-owned companies will gain traction as people seek to associate for mutual benefit. I believe this collective approach will help people—who more and more are feeling like they've lost control over their economic lives—address a number of issues, from income equality to work benefits.

These ownership approaches also help people obtain a higher need, that of wanting to be part of something bigger than themselves. I believe this need will be hastened by technology: from the Internet's penchant to open-source solutions to social media's capacity to organize groups to independent computer programmers' embrace of working together around areas of shared interest.

While people might not have the capacity or desire to own a business, they do want a stake and voice in things. Co-ops and ESOPS provide a solution here.

There's an existing template for this, and not a small one at that—there are currently more than 30,000 worker-owned cooperatives in this country, with collective revenues exceeding $650 billion.[58] As for models of employee-owned companies, there are more than 7,000 in the U.S., with 13.5 million participants. They range from Publix supermarkets, with more than 180,000 employee owners, to the world's largest consulting engineering firm, CH2M Hill (20,000 employee owners), and the maker of Fat Tire Amber Ale, New Belgium Brewing (nearly 800 employee owners).

It's interesting to note that research from the National Center for Employee Ownership finds that employee-owned companies perform better than traditional companies, and they deliver more jobs over the long run, too.[59]

Yes, both are small portions of the overall economy, but look for them to make significant gains in number and influence.

As for women, no news here—there's a huge and troubling gender gap in corporate leadership, as the percentages of women CEOs, senior executives, and board members come nowhere near matching the percentage of women in the workforce. But this will change mightily, as the purpose-driven movement, combined with social technology, will give rise to increasing influence for female entrepreneurs and corporate executives.

In 2016, 5 percent of the Fortune 500 CEOs were women, while just 15 percent of senior executives were female.[60] Corporate boards fare a bit better, perhaps because of shareholder activism, hovering around 18 percent of the Fortune 1000.[61]

I'd look for at least 25 percent—and hopefully more—of this country's CEOs to be female in the next 10 years, with senior executives and board members coming closer to approximating the overall gender complexion of the workplace.

Here's why this change will occur: Women simply get the purpose-driven movement far better than men, in my estimation, and will see long-overdue leadership gains because of it.

Statistically, women donate, volunteer, and advocate for causes at rates that far exceed those of men. They drive the dominant share of consumer spending, and they actually hold the majority of wealth in this country. In my experience, they listen better, excel in collaborative settings, and are able to work more effectively in holistic environments considering multiple outcomes. Where men might tend to narrowly focus around one result (say, profit), women often have broader perspectives and round out financial profit with the addition of others (people and planet, for instance).

Combined with their communication skills and ability to navigate social networks occasioned by new technology, I believe all of these factors combine to make women ideal leaders in a purpose-driven model of business.

Of course, that's purely unsupported opinion, but if you're looking for evidence, I can offer up one powerful example that might surprise you: General Motors, led by female CEO Mary Barra. In 2016, GM became the first major industrial company in the United States to reach gender parity on its board with a composition that is 50/50 female and male.

I'd look for companies to become more competitive by mirroring GM's approach. It's about time.

KEY POINTS

- Certifications for environmental and social performance won't be a choice; they will become universal and mandated by the marketplace in the future

- Sustainability reports will become history, giving way to reports that indicate all key performance indicators of a company, from financial to environmental and social

- Everything that can be given a number and rated will be rated—even in our personal lives

- A new breed of nonprofits will thrive as social enterprises incorporating market-based strategies and revenue models

- Companies will augment traditional philanthropy by making more impact investments directly in social enterprises

- Workers will have more voice in the companies where they work, and women will find new opportunity to make business smarter for the benefit of everyone

"

"Life's most persistent and urgent question is, 'What are you doing for others?'"

Martin Luther King, Jr.

CHAPTER 13
WE ARE ALL SOCIAL ENTREPRENEURS

There's much to be hopeful about in the rise of socially conscious companies around the world.

And it's not just my generally sunny optimism; this trend is backed by substantive statistics.

Consider:

The first public benefit corporation legislation in the United States was passed in Maryland in 2010. Today, there are more than 4,000 public benefit corporations in this country.

The nonprofit B Lab certified its first B Corps in 2007. By the time our firm, Oliver Russell, was certified in January 2012, there were 299 B Corps in the world. By mid-2017, the number of B Corps globally increased to more than 2,100 companies. While this is still a small community, this growth rate demonstrates an accelerating trajectory that harbors good things for the future of social impact.

The B Corp Movement is Growing

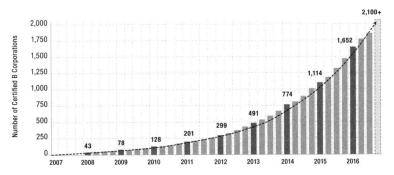

Perhaps the strongest validation for this movement comes from financial investors funneling more money into companies specifically because they deliver positive social and environmental impact alongside profit. In 2015, a study of 126 institutions by the Global Impact Investing Network showed that this group had made more than $15 billion (U.S.) in impact investments in 2015—and planned to increase this amount by 16 percent in 2016.[62]

PARTNERSHIPS WITH PURPOSE

On the ground, exciting events are taking place. Last year, Patagonia committed to donating all its Black Friday sales to grassroots environmental groups. It registered $10 million in sales that day, more than three times the previous year's Black Friday totals. This not only provided necessary fuel for local nonprofits, it demonstrated this approach is a huge motivation for the consumers who rang up that record sales day.

Exciting partnerships are taking place between like-minded, socially conscious companies. Ben & Jerry's partnered with New Belgium Brewing to collaborate on two new beers (Chocolate Chip Cookie Dough Ale and Salted Caramel Brownie Brown Ale, in case you're thirsty). By joining forces to create new products, they leveraged two powerful brand names and customer followings to increase sales and awareness for socially conscious businesses.

Internationally, organizations such as B1G1,[63] an online giving platform for small businesses, are successfully building communities with
thousands of business members demonstrating that the act of giving
back is good for the world—and good for business.

COME TO THE AID OF YOUR COUNTRY

"Now is the time for all good social entrepreneurs to come to the aid
of their country."

I don't know why, but this phrase from long ago came into my
mind lately, and it stuck. It's a slight riff on a quote often mistakenly
attributed to the American patriot Patrick Henry. In reality, however,
it was the work of an instructor who came up with it as a typing drill
way back in 1867.

Indeed, now is the time for all good social entrepreneurs to come
to the aid of their country, and when I say country, I don't mean
sovereign nation—I mean the world. As in the time is now not only
to do good, but also to look at the world as if it were your country.

And when I say social entrepreneur, friend, I'm not limiting the
universe to businesspeople.

I mean you.

I mean all of us.

While there is a lot of talent and capital directed toward using
business to make positive social and environmental change, I'm
feeling a heightened sense of urgency.

This book is directed at social entrepreneurs who want to build purpose-driven businesses to develop inspiring products, services, and business models benefitting society. Now, more than ever, we need to foster people using business for a higher purpose. We need to create businesses dedicated to providing public benefit along with bottom-line financial profit.

But here's the thing: You don't have to start or own a business to participate. There's a broader definition of the name "social entrepreneur" that includes each of us.

HOW YOU SPEND YOUR MONEY MATTERS

Let me start by saying money isn't everything—but it IS the thing I'm going to talk about here.

Where, and how, we spend our money matters. In a way, you cast your vote at the cash register or the e-commerce checkout. You're buying a product, but you're also voting for the company that produces it.

Taken together with the purchases of other like-minded shoppers who are driven by purpose, consumer spending provides the energy for social impact and a refashioning of the corporate charter. While none of us has billions of dollars or employs legions of lobbyists, it turns out each of us can use our resources to change the way the world works. No matter how small.

Look for third-party certifications when you're making a purchase. As discussed in this book, there's not yet a unified symbol for corporate social impact and behavior, but there are a number of certifications that can be helpful in guiding your purchasing decisions.

Refashion your purchasing as an opportunity to become your own sleuth and explore a company's policies and behavior. Now, I know you're busy and convenience is part of the value equation, but you can find many compelling companies and stories if you take a moment to search a little bit.

For instance, if you're thinking about a pair of women's work pants from Carhartt, take just a moment in your search and you may discover a company like Red Ants Pants—one that gets rave reviews for the durability and fit of its products and has an intentional mission to develop and expand leadership roles for women, preserve and support working family farms and ranches, and enrich and promote rural communities. They're a "human" brand, one with flesh and bones and emotion and real-world impact. That's a recipe for a more meaningful purchase.

ONLINE TOOLS FOR ETHICAL OPTIONS

Seek out online tools to assist you in your effort. For instance, a new tool recently arrived on the scene that can help you make ethical purchasing decisions. DoneGood[64] creates a browser extension for Chrome that makes it easier to discover businesses on a mission to improve the world. When you're shopping online, the DoneGood extension alerts you to ethical, sustainable companies offering similar products to what you're currently shopping. Pretty easy, pretty sweet.

The point here is yes, this type of shopping takes more time; not much, but some, though you'll be enriched for your minimal efforts by finding companies and products that are generative—they produce more positive energy than they consume (energy here being a metaphor). When you intentionally spend your money with a social enterprise, you become, by extension, a social entrepreneur. And that feels pretty good.

WHERE WE WORK MATTERS

Like they say, time is money. We live in a world of limited resources, and the most precious resource you have is, well, you.

So if you want to change the world, why not put your shoulder to the wheel at a company actively working to solve social and environmental problems through its products, services, or business model? You've got gifts that are uniquely your own—perspective, skills, experience, passion, and TALENT!

Traditionally, you'd accomplish this by working for a nonprofit organization, which is a satisfying way to invest in your work life. But now you have the option of achieving similar outcomes in the for-profit world by working for a social enterprise.

Sure, changing jobs isn't as easy as flipping the switch on your everyday spending. But there are increasingly numerous opportunities to spend your workdays creating impact and leaving your job at day's end feeling that you are contributing to a solution rather than being part of the problem. From personal experience and the anecdotes of others, I can tell you this brings a completely new sense of meaning to the half of your waking day you spend working.

You'll need to make a plan and start by researching the types of jobs that are available. Here are several resources that can help you in your search.

Rework - A progressive recruiting firm that matches mission-driven talent to the world's socially innovative organizations.[65]

NextBillion - The job board for this community of business leaders, social entrepreneurs, and NGO managers.[66]

Social Good Jobs - A service of the Green Jobs Network to help locate jobs in social entrepreneurship.[67]

B Corps Job Board - Employment opportunities with Certified B Corps—companies using business to solve social and environmental problems.[68]

Idealist - Connects "idealists"—people who want to do good—with job opportunities for action and collaboration.[69]

A CHALLENGE TO MY FELLOW SOCIAL ENTREPRENEURS

Lastly, I'll offer a challenge to my fellow social enterprises.

Your purchasing department has an unsung, indirect, yet immensely powerful role to play in creating social change. As social entrepreneurs, we need to be every bit the conscious consumer as the discerning Millennial when considering business purchases.

And here's why: Our business purchasing can foster significant change by investing our mission-driven dollars with other mission-driven businesses.

Here are a few questions to consider. Do you have other social enterprises on your purchasing roster? Are you including local suppliers in the equation? If not—why? You'll find that with minimally more assessment and effort—really a little bit of thought is all it takes— you can employ your purchasing to leverage a powerful economic multiplier, funneling your supply-chain spending to other social enterprises and purpose-driven companies.

Perhaps it's easier to think of yourself as a venture capitalist or an impact investor—when you are purchasing on behalf of your business, you are making small investments in other businesses, playing an important part in a virtuous cycle with tremendous impact.

If all else is equal (price, quality, service, convenience, which often are at relative parity), this should be an easy choice. Make it and you'll achieve three objectives: You'll provide much-needed fuel for a kindred company; open doors to creative collaborations, partnerships, and reciprocal spending; and offer a strong statement of moral support to another social entrepreneur.

OUR TIME IS NOW

We've been banding together for security and socialization since humans first roamed the earth. Now is the time for each of us, as social entrepreneurs and as conscious consumers, to roll up our sleeves and our spending, along with our voices, into a force that generates more positive energy in the world.

All of this requires some thought, but not that much. It takes shifts in behavior, which is tougher, but not like putting a rocket into space. It can all come to pass through our own individual and collective commitments, and it's these small, daily actions of thousands of businesses and millions of individuals that can change and save our world.

That's what it will take—simply a realization that we are all social entrepreneurs.

So rise up, people, *Rise Up*.

KEY POINTS

- Critical measures such as Benefit Corporation formation and global flow of capital to impact investing are rising sharply

- Spend your hard-earned money with companies that share your social and environmental values

- Where you work matters—put your talent to work at a social enterprise

- Social enterprises should band together to maximize their resources and impact

- We are all social entrepreneurs

ACTION PLAN

Here's a quick reminder of the key items you'll need to act upon or consider when forming your social enterprise. These items are not sequential and will often have areas of overlap.

1. MENTOR
Find a mentor who has experience with the business of social enterprise.

2. PURPOSE
Craft your purpose statement, the change you want to make in the world.

3. VALUES
Determine your values, the principles and ideals by which every person at your company will live.

5. MANIFESTO
Create a manifesto as a public declaration of your company's purpose and values. While you're at it, start scripting your brand story, key marketing messages, and tone of voice, plus the design of your brand identity.

6. LEGAL STATUS
Determine whether a formal legal status, such as Benefit Corporation or L3C, is appropriate for your venture. The office of your secretary of state is a good starting point.

7. PEOPLE AND WORKPLACE

Think purposefully about the type of workplace you'd like to create. This includes policies and employee benefits. Be cognizant that these also have important cost implications to consider.

8. CERTIFICATION

Investigate third-party certification programs such as Certified B Corporations, and assess other avenues to help you measure the sustainability of your company.

9. BANKING RELATIONSHIPS

You'll need a bank—be sure to talk with credit unions and local independent banks. This is an example of one data point taken into consideration if you plan to become a Certified B Corporation.

10. LEGAL ASSISTANCE

Find an attorney who has experience with social enterprises, Benefit Corporations, Certified B Corps, or L3Cs. Ask other social entrepreneurs for recommendations.

11. SUPPLIERS

Start with a mindset for partnerships with other like-minded social entrepreneurs; remember that every time your business makes a purchase, it has the ability to create change.

12. FUNDING

From Day 1, create a long-term investor plan that makes sense and provides flexibility in the future. Don't hesitate to seek advice from a pro even if you don't currently require financing.

13. ANNUAL REPORT

It's a good idea to prepare an annual report after your fiscal year-end. So be thinking along the way what you'll want to include; don't wait until the end when it's too late to start measuring the metrics you'll need.

14. QUESTIONS

I'll be happy to help if you have questions or direct you to someone who can be of assistance. My email address is rstoddard@oliverrussell.com, and you can also connect with me on my website.[70]

RESOURCES

Good news! You're not in this alone, and there are a number of quality resources available to help as you change the world by creating a socially conscious business.

GET YOUR BOOK CLUB ON

The Purpose Economy: How Your Desire for Impact, Personal Growth, and Community is Changing the World by Aaron Hurst. Aaron provides a compelling case study for overall changes in the economy that are being driven by people's desire to obtain meaning through their work.

The B Corp Handbook: How to Use Business as a Force for Good by Ryan Honeyman. If you're interested in certifying as a B Corp, listen to Ryan—he's one of the foremost experts and has created an easy-to-use guide that walks you through the process.

Content Chemistry: An Illustrated Handbook for Content Marketing by Andy Crestodina. One of the most effective ways to share your company's story of purpose is through content marketing on the web, and Andy (of B Corp Orbit Media) is one of the best teachers.

Designing for Sustainability: A Guide to Building Greener Digital Products by Tim Frick. This is a little off-topic, but so much of the good accomplished by social enterprises happens on the Internet—Tim's book shows how to minimize negative effects.

B the Change Media. A multi-platform media company providing articles, news, reports, and other information across the social enterprise spectrum, delivered via print magazine and the web.[71]

THESE GROUPS ARE YOUR FRIENDS

B Lab—the nonprofit B Lab operates the assessment program to certify B Corporations. Its website provides a wealth of resources and information that can help you on your path, regardless of whether you choose to certify or not.[72]

Impact Hub Global Network—an innovation lab/business incubator/ co-working space for social entrepreneurs. Impact Hub has facilities around the world where members collaborate and grow the impact of their work.[73]

Social Capital Markets—you'll find your tribe at "Socap," an annual rendezvous in San Francisco that brings together social entrepreneurs and impact investors.[74]

Universities—from the Skoll Center for Social Entrepreneurship at Oxford and Yale University's School of Management to the West Coast trio of Stanford, the Haas School of Business at Cal-Berkeley, and the Presidio Graduate School on the West Coast, business schools on many college campuses are becoming hot beds for social enterprise. You'll even find burgeoning responsible business initiatives at smaller schools such as the College of Charleston and Boise State University.

GO OLD SCHOOL

Finally, if you have a question, and you can't find the answer on the web or in a book—be human! Try the old-school way of directly contacting a social entrepreneur—in your town, in Singapore, on the web, wherever. I've found that people in this business of purpose are incredibly open and welcoming, and quite willing to provide mentorship. And they'll likely gain as much from the conversation as you will. So go ahead and make that call, now. The world is waiting.

RUSS STODDARD

Russ began his career as a river guide before entering the corporate world where he has become recognized as an expert working at the confluence of business and social responsibility.

He is the founder and president of Oliver Russell, a public benefit corporation that builds brands for purpose-driven companies whose products, services or business models benefit society.

Russ is a leader in the Certified B Corporation community, a new classification of companies that use the power of business to solve social and environmental issues. He has received awards for lifetime achievements in community service from the American Advertising Federation, the YMCA, and his alma mater, the University of Puget Sound.

He lives in beautiful Boise, Idaho, with his wife, Sarah, and their standard poodle, Roux.

ENDNOTES

1   *Ad Age Online.* (2013, March 7).

2   *Deloitte, Culture of Purpose: A business imperative.* (2013).
    Core Beliefs and Culture Survey.

3   "Big Business Speaks Up on Social Issues" (2016, April 17).
    The Wall Street Journal.

4   "Big Business Speaks Up on Social Issues" (2016, April 17).
    The Wall Street Journal.

5   http://cbey.yale.edu/programs-research/an-entrepre-
    neur's-guide-to-certified-b-corporations-and-benefit-
    corporations

6   https://www.bcorporation.net

7   https://www.bcorporation.net/community/oliver-russell-
    associates

8   http://www.goodwellworld.com

9   http://www.thesroinetwork.org

10 https://www.theguardian.com/sustainable-business/2015/
    jan/29/businesses-learn-language-of-natural-capital-2015

11 https://ecotone-partners.com

12 http://consciousbrands.com

13 http://www.lifteconomy.com

14 https://www.globalreporting.org/information/sustainability-reporting/Pages/default.aspx

15 https://iris.thegiin.org

16 https://thegiin.org

17 http://www.un.org/sustainabledevelopment/sustainable-development-goals/

18 https://www.fairwear.org/about/

19 http://www.onepercentfortheplanet.org

20 http://b-analytics.net/giirs-ratings

21 (2015, 2016). B Lab + B the Change Media.

22 "Best Places to Work in Idaho." (2015). *Micro Employers.*

23 http://spring.is

24 http://www.hubventures.org

25 http://goodcompanyventures.org

26 http://www.unltdusa.org

27 http://unreasonableinstitute.org

28 http://www.ycombinator.com

29 http://www.techstars.com

30 http://www.investorscircle.net

31 http://www.enableimpact.com

32 http://www.toniic.com

33 https://angel.co/social-entrepreneurship-1

34 http://www.kaporcapital.com

35 https://a16z.com

36 http://www.aera.vc

37 http://www.lifteconomy.com/forceforgood/

38 https://straydogcapital.com

39 https://www.omidyar.com

40 https://chanzuckerberg.com

41 Walker, D. (2017, April 5). Unleashing Endowments the Next Great Challenge for Philanthropy [Blog]. Retrieved from http://www.fordfoundation.org/ideas/equals-change-blog/posts/unleashing-the-power-of-endowments-the-next-great-challenge-for-philanthropy

42 Polk, S. (2017, March 10). I left finance because I wanted to make a difference. Non-profit work never did the trick. Los Angeles Times. Retrieved from http://www.latimes.com/opinion/op-ed/la-oe-polk-the-case-for-profit-social-enterprise-20170312-story.html

43 http://www.icba.org/home

44 http://beneficialstatebank.com

45 https://www.newresourcebank.com

46 http://springbankny.com

47 https://sunrisebanks.com

48 http://rsfsocialfinance.org/get-funding/funding-overview/

49 https://www.regrained.com

50 https://www.linkedin.com/groups/120110/profile

51 https://www.linkedin.com/company/cause-marketing-forum

52 http://www.csrwire.com

53 http://www.triplepundit.com

54 https://www.prlog.org

55 http://www.huffingtonpost.com/news/purpose--profit/

56 http://www.forbes.com/social-entrepreneurship/#640c3dc
    07cf9

57 http://wpabeer.com

58 Time. (2016, July 11).

59 Entrepreneur. (2015, February 23).

60 The Washington Post. (2015, June 4).

61 Fortune. (2015, January 13).

62 Global Investing Impact Network 2016 Annual Impact
    Investor Survey.

63 https://www.b1g1.com/businessforgood/

64 https://donegood.co

65 http://www.rework.jobs

66 http://nextbillion.net/jobs/

67 http://socialgoodjobs.org

68 https://www.bcorporation.net/community/jobs-board

69 http://www.idealist.org/search/v2/?search_type=job

70 http://www.russstoddard.com

71 http://www.bthechange.com

72 https://www.bcorporation.net/what-are-b-corps/about-b-lab

73 http://www.impacthub.net

74 http://socialcapitalmarkets.net

75 https://www.b1g1.com/businessforgood/

INDEX

YOUR PURCHASE MAKES A DIFFERENCE

Every time someone buys this book, a child in Cambodia receives access to textbooks. This is accomplished through a partnership with B1G1,[75] one of the world's leading online platforms for business giving.

elevate
publishing

DELIVERING TRANSFORMATIVE MESSAGES
TO THE WORLD

Visit www.elevatepub.com for our latest offerings.

NO TREES WERE HARMED IN THE MAKING OF THIS BOOK.

Okay, so a few did make the ultimate sacrifice.

In order to steward our environment, we are partnered with *Plant With Purpose*, to plant a tree for every tree that paid the price for the printing of this book.

To learn more, visit www.elevatepub.com/about